REIMAGINE CALLING, OCCUPATION, PASSION, OPPORTUNITY

TROY A. EVANS

Troy Evans

2305 East Paris

Grand Rapids Michigan 49546

troyevansspeaks@gmail.com

Cover design by Erika Bland

Printed in United States

First Printing: 2024

Library of Congress Cataloging-in-Publication Data

Evans, Troy.

COPO   REIMAGINE   CALLING   OCCUPATION   PASSION
OPPORTUNITY

ISBN: 979-8-9915733-0-6, 979-8-9915733-1-3

Manufactured in United States

TABLE OF CONTENTS

INTRODUCTION

I remember connecting with one of my friends, Rob, who is an absolute genius. He was some years younger than me but mentored me in many ways. I don't remember what led to the conversation about clarifying what God has called everyone to do. He wrote 4 circles on a paper and went on to talk about COPO (Calling, Occupation, Passion, Opportunity). I was completely blown away by this concept and started using it with pastors, business owners, leaders, youth, and young adults all across the country. As I started using it, I realized that I needed to remix it so that it made sense to teens, leaders, and the everyday person who is trying to figure out what their purpose is.

Everyone that I've discipled, coached, or mentored has heard of this life-altering tool more times than they probably would like. I can't help but use this tool as God has used COPO as a guide to help leaders, business owners, pastors, and even gang members define and gain greater clarity on their God-given purpose.

I contacted Rob fourteen years later to thank him for this investment and asked where he got the concept from. He said he did not remember and assumed it was possibly one of his mentors.

So, I have no idea if Rob ate bad pizza one night or if his mentor gave it to him. I am just forever thankful and wanted to share my version of this tool through the lens of a few wild characters.

This book is crafted to help you identify and adopt your unique purpose in life. Each component of COPO is essential in helping you live a life aligned with your true purpose.

Fourteen years ago, when I started sharing COPO with people, I noticed how this simple concept could change people's perspectives. It wasn't just about identifying what they should do with their lives; it was about connecting the dots between their calling, occupation, passion, and the opportunities that lay before them.

It became clear that COPO had the power to give people clarity on their next steps, regardless of where they were in life. That's what made it such an invaluable tool—not just for pastors or business leaders, but for anyone wanting to discover their true purpose.

The beauty of COPO is its flexibility. It doesn't dictate a single path but helps you figure out how you can find the balance between your calling, occupation, passion, and opportunities. And when you do, that's where you find your purpose. Some people I've mentored were amazed at how simple it could be to break down something as complex as life's purpose into these four components. Others needed more time to digest it and see how each part fit into their own life. But, in the end, COPO consistently gave people the clarity and direction they needed.

What makes COPO special is that it's not just a one-size-fits-all model. It's adaptable to wherever you are in your journey. You don't have to be a leader of a church, a business owner, or someone with a traditional leadership role to benefit from it. COPO can guide anyone —from students to parents to professionals—by giving them a framework to think about their life and purpose in a more intentional way.

Above all, this book is not about following my exact steps or even Rob's original idea. It's about you finding the steps that align with who you are and what the Lord has called you to do. Each of us has a different purpose, unique passions, and a calling that only we can fulfill. I hope this book helps you discover yours.

As you move through the book, I'll share my personal journey and stories from people around me to help you understand COPO very well. Some of these stories are funny, some are heartbreaking, but all of them are real. I believe you'll see a bit of yourself in each one and be inspired to dig deeper into your own journey.

My hope is that this book doesn't just give you ideas but equips you with a practical tool to help you rise up and step into your God-given purpose. I'm not promising that the process will be easy or quick, but I can assure you it will be worth it. There's something powerful about living with purpose—when you wake up each day knowing that what you're doing matters, not just for you, but for the people around you. That's the life I want for you, and I believe COPO can help get you there.

Chapter One
CALLING

When I first heard about the word "calling," I wasn't sure what it really meant. Like many people, I assumed it was something reserved for pastors, missionaries, or those involved in full-time ministry. But over time, I realized that calling isn't just for a select group of people—it's for everyone. God has a plan for each of our lives, and that plan includes a specific purpose. Discovering your calling is about figuring out what the Lord wants you to do and living in alignment with that purpose.

As a Christian, the question takes on even deeper meaning because you know that the Lord has created you with intention. There's a unique calling in your life, but how do you figure out what that is? How do you go from wandering through life to walking confidently in your God-given purpose?

Your calling is the unique way God wants to use you to impact the world. This is bigger than just a job or career—it's about how your life contributes to God's kingdom. Some people feel called to ministry, but that's not the only type of calling. You could be called to use your gifts in business, education, the arts, or any other area of life. Your calling is what drives you, the core reason why you're here. But what does the word "Calling" truly mean?

> *"Discovering your calling is about figuring out what the Lord wants you to do and living in alignment with that purpose."*

A calling is more than just a career or a job. It's not about the position you hold or the title you have. It's about the role that the Lord has created you to play on earth. When we talk about calling, we are talking about something that goes beyond our everyday responsibilities and taps into our deepest sense of purpose. It's the thing that gives your life meaning, the reason why you are here, and what the Lord has uniquely equipped you to do.

We are all created with a purpose. The Lord has already prepared the path for us to walk on; we just need to discover it. Your calling isn't something you have to invent or create from scratch. It's something that God has already placed in you, waiting to be uncovered. God has called each of us to do the following.

CALL TO SURRENDER

We are all called to surrender to Jesus because He knows the best for us. You know, life has a way of leading us down paths we never intended to take. We often find ourselves entangled in the pursuit of things we think will bring us happiness—whether it's money, status, relationships, or personal achievements, only to find ourselves feeling more lost than ever. But how often do we sit down and ask ourselves these questions? Is this really what I want? *Is this what I need?*

Sometimes, no matter how much we try to keep everything together, we just hit that breaking point. And when we do, we're faced with a choice: keep struggling to control it all or just let go and surrender to Jesus. That was me a few years ago. I'll share that story with you soon, but for now, let's keep going.

Letting go of control and trusting Jesus? It can totally change your life. It's not about giving up; it's about finding a new direction with the Lord. Some people think surrender means weakness. They've trained themselves to believe that success comes from always hustling, pushing harder, and never letting up. But honestly, my real strength is recognizing that we can't do it all by ourselves. That's where surrender to the Lord comes in.

"Surrender doesn't mean throwing in the towel. It's more like realizing you don't have to carry the weight of everything on your shoulders."

There's a freedom that comes with admitting you need help and a sense of peace when you let Jesus take the lead.

This kinda reminds me of that 2016 Marvel movie Doctor Strange. Remember Stephen Strange? He was this big-shot, cocky neurosurgeon who thought he had life all figured out, totally in control. Then boom—a tragic accident messed up his hands, and just like that, his career was over.

He tried everything to get his life back on track. Nothing worked. So, desperate, he went looking for healing in some strange, far-off place. That's where he met the Ancient One. She hit him with the truth: to really grow, he had to let go of his need for control and trust in something bigger—forces he couldn't even begin to understand.

At first, Strange wasn't having it. He fought the idea of surrendering, much like people resist surrendering to Jesus, thinking it makes them weak. But when Strange finally let go and accepted that he

Now, surrender can mean different things for different people, depending on where you're at in life. For some, it might mean stepping away from chasing success. For others, it's about letting go of toxic relationships or giving up the need to control things that are just out of your hands. No matter what it looks like for you, surrender can open up a whole new way of living, one filled with peace and purpose.

But you must understand that surrender requires trust. It means trusting that even when things don't go our way, God is still working things out. It's believing that there's more to life than what's happening right in front of us, and sometimes, the best thing we can do is step back and let God take control. I get it, though—it's not easy, especially in a world that's all about grinding, being productive, and always doing something. But sometimes, the most productive thing we can do is pause, reflect, and give it over to Jesus.

For us as believers, surrender is the path to real peace. It doesn't mean we stop taking action or being responsible; it just means we learn when to act and when to step aside. When we surrender to the Lord, we often gain clarity on what really matters. And when we stop trying to control everything, we make room for something new—whether it's a fresh insight or a new direction in life.

Surrender can actually be empowering. When we let go of what's been holding us back, we create space for growth. Sometimes, we can be stuck in old habits or relationships that don't serve us because we're scared to let go. But when we finally surrender, we can break free and move forward, more aligned with who we're meant to be.

The hardest part of surrender, though, is fear of the unknown. We hold onto what we are used to, even if it's not good for us because we're afraid of what might happen if we let go. But that's where the magic of surrendering to Jesus happens. It's in those moments of uncertainty that we grow the most. When we decide to walk with the Lord in faith, we discover strengths we didn't even know we had and possibilities we couldn't have imagined. I didn't know the Lord had such a big plan for my life until I surrendered to Him. And ever since I did, I've had zero regrets.

Another thing to remember is that surrender goes hand-in-hand with acceptance. It's about accepting where we are, even if it's not where we want to be right now. Life might not be going according to our plan, but that doesn't mean it's not going exactly how it's supposed to in God's plan. When we accept our current situation, that's when real change can start.

Let me share my salvation journey with you and how surrendering to Jesus has left me with no regrets.

I was knee-deep in gang life, just drifting from one chaotic situation to another. But everything took a turn when I moved from Grand Rapids to Detroit and found myself at this huge church with my girlfriend. To be honest, I wasn't really into church at all. I was just going along because she convinced me to give it a shot.

Then came that service—oh man, I was not interested in hearing another preacher talking this weird Christian talk. But out of nowhere, this man came out speaking in regular language, talking about a very real God. His message hit me like a brick in a way I never saw coming. In my book, *The Way of the Man*, I talk about how there isn't a clear-cut guide to being a man in America. There are no rights of passage, as we see in many cultures. Leaving me to figure this out one failure at a time. For years, I thought being a man meant racking up conquests with women, stacking money, and showing how hard I could be. But that day, all of that was thrown into question. I was in a really vulnerable place, and I learned that's where God typically steps in to do His best work "when we're out of options and desperate for something we can't even name."

It reminded me of the Apostle Paul when he was in Athens (Acts 17). The locals were talking about this "unknown God," and Paul jumped in to clarify who that was. That was me, searching for something, even if I didn't realize it was the God of the universe I was longing for.

So there I was, sitting in this packed church with all these feelings swirling around. I had just come out of a rough few months, battling PTSD and trying to drown my pain in alcohol. Now I'm stuck sitting here with all those people; it feels like it is just me and the Lord. I was desperate for Him. I recognized I suck, He is awesome, and I was in desperate need of His grace more than anything.

Then, the preacher said something that might have seemed ordinary to others, but it struck a chord with me: "It's not enough for you to just be a man; it's time for you to stand up and be God's man." In that moment, everything clicked. I realized that everything I had done up to that point was the opposite of what it meant to be a real man. I needed to figure out how to be an honorable, godly man.

Though there were adult males around me, I didn't have anyone to show me God's way. I definitely didn't want to be that guy who just sat in church, tossed money in the offering plate, and didn't make any real impact on the world. I wanted more than that. That day, I accepted my first calling—to become a disciple of this Jesus. In that altar call, with about 300 people around me, I looked over and saw my girlfriend—she must have sensed that unknown God, too. She realized His power was way beyond anything we could imagine, even more powerful than our love for each other.

That day, she surrendered her life to Jesus, too, and we both ended up in tears. Fast forward three decades later, and she's not just my girlfriend anymore—she's now my wife, my best friend, and my partner in this wild journey of life, LaDawn Evans. We haven't stopped crying or celebrating since!

Surrendering to Jesus is not just a single-time event. It's a continuous journey. You will see this as we continue in this book. Even after that great moment in church, where I surrendered my life to Jesus, I've had to make the choice to surrender again and again.

Life has thrown plenty of challenges my way—some small, others life-changing—but each time, I've had to remind myself to let go of my need for control and trust in God's plan. This is not easy. There are moments when I've been tempted to take matters into my own hands, thinking I know best. But every time I try to do things my way, I end up right back where I started: frustrated, lost, and in need of God's grace.

The truth is, surrender doesn't mean life suddenly becomes smooth sailing. It doesn't mean you won't face struggles or that everything will instantly fall into place. But what surrender does is shift your perspective. It allows you to face life's challenges with a different mindset, one that isn't focused on controlling every outcome but is instead grounded in faith and trust. You start to see difficulties not as setbacks but as opportunities for growth. You begin to realize that even in the midst of challenges, Jesus is still in control, working things out for your good.

Over the years, I've come to see that surrender is less about giving up and more about giving in—to God's will, to His timing, and to His greater plan for my life. It's about releasing my grip on the things I can't control and focusing on what I can: my faith, my attitude, and my obedience to His word. When you live in a constant state of surrender, you begin to experience a deeper sense of peace. That's not to say there won't be moments of doubt or fear, but in those moments, you can lean on Jesus, knowing He has everything under control.

I've also learned that surrender often requires sacrifice. There have been times when I've had to let go of things I thought were good for me—dreams, desires, or opportunities—only to realize later that God had something better in store for me.

It's hard to let go of something when you don't know what's coming next. But that's where faith comes in. Faith is trusting that even when you can't see the whole picture, God is working behind the scenes, setting things up for your good.

If I could give you one piece of advice, it would be this: don't wait until you hit rock bottom to surrender. Don't wait until you've exhausted every option and have nowhere else to turn. Surrender now. Trust the Lord now. It doesn't matter where you are in life or what you're going through; Jesus is ready to step in and take control, but you have to let Him.

Looking back on my own journey, I'm grateful for every moment of surrender, even the difficult ones. They've brought me closer to Jesus, strengthened my faith, and helped me become the man He created me to be. And I believe the same can be true for you, too.

CALL TO ACTION

In life, it's easy to get caught up in routine and comfort, focusing on the predictable and familiar. We often settle into patterns that feel safe, but deep down, many of us feel a tug—an inkling that there's something more we're meant to do. This feeling, this call to action, can sometimes come from unexpected places and challenge us to step out of our comfort zones into a world of uncertainty and growth.

A call to action isn't just about responding to an external push; it's about recognizing an internal nudge that's urging us to embrace our purpose. It's about moving from a place of whatever happens to a place where I have to do something. This call often arrives when we least expect it, breaking through our normal routines and challenging us to reconsider our roles and responsibilities in the world.

Imagine you're living your life, doing what you've always done when suddenly, you're faced with a message or an event that shakes things up. It might not be dramatic or earth-shattering, but it's enough to make you stop and think. You might hear a compelling message that resonates with you or perhaps a conversation with someone who sees something in you that you've never noticed before. This moment can be the beginning of something transformative in your life.

The essence of a call to action is that it asks us to respond, to take steps beyond what we're comfortable with. It's not about waiting for the perfect conditions or the right time; it's about stepping up when the opportunity arises. This call often demands that we look beyond our limitations and embrace new challenges with an open heart.

For some, this might mean taking on a leadership role, pursuing a new career, or starting a project that's been on the back burner. For others, it might involve a shift in how we interact with those around us, how we serve our community, or how we align our lives with our values. The key is recognizing that this call is an invitation to grow and contribute in ways we hadn't imagined before.

It's easy to dismiss these calls as coincidences or fleeting thoughts. After all, responding to a call to action can be challenging. It might mean stepping into unknown territory, facing our insecurities, or challenging the status quo. But often, it's in these very moments of discomfort that we find our true potential. By stepping out of our comfort zones, we give ourselves the chance to discover what we're really capable of.

When you're faced with a call to action, you have a choice. You can choose to stay where you are, continuing with the usual but unremarkable routine. Or, you can choose to embrace the call, even if it's scary or unclear. Taking action doesn't mean you have to have everything figured out. It means you're willing to take a step of faith, trusting that the journey will reveal itself as you move forward.

One powerful aspect of responding to a call to action is the sense of purpose it brings. When you act on a call, you align your actions with something greater than yourself. This can be incredibly fulfilling, giving you direction and meaning that goes beyond daily tasks and responsibilities. It's about making a difference in ways that resonate deeply with who you are and what you value.

Sometimes, the call to action requires us to be proactive. It's not always about waiting for someone else to recognize our potential or offer us an opportunity. Often, it's about taking the initiative, exploring new possibilities, and making the most of the opportunities that come our way. This proactive stance helps us to take control of our destinies and shape our futures in meaningful ways. Taking action can also be a catalyst for growth. When we step out of our comfort zones, we challenge ourselves to learn and adapt. We might discover new skills, develop new perspectives, or meet people who inspire and support us. This growth can be transformative, leading to a greater understanding of ourselves and a more profound connection with the world around us.

Moreover, responding to a call to action often leads to unexpected rewards. While the journey might be challenging, the outcomes can be incredibly rewarding. We might find new passions, form lasting relationships, or achieve goals we never thought possible. These rewards are often the result of embracing the unknown and taking bold steps forward.

So, how can you recognize and respond to a call to action in your own life? Start by paying attention to the moments that spark a sense of excitement or curiosity. These might be hints that there's something more you're meant to explore. Reflect on what resonates with you and what you're passionate about. Look for opportunities to take small steps toward these interests, and don't be afraid to embrace the discomfort that comes with change.

Let me share this wild story about my second calling with you. So, one day, this random guy shows up at our church, and he doesn't know me at all. He preached a message that, honestly, I can't even remember. But what I do remember is me just strolling down the aisle, chatting with people, just kicking it. Then, out of nowhere, the pastor points at me and goes, "Hey, you!" I'm thinking, "Me?" He says, "The Lord is telling me you're called to be a preacher." And I'm like, "Wait, what?" He wasn't just talking about preaching, though; he meant being a pastor, like a shepherd. And if you know me, you'd know I wasn't exactly the poster child for future pastors. I didn't speak well, I didn't read much, and honestly, I didn't know jack about church stuff. So, I was totally caught off guard!

I was still wrapping my head around all of this, trying to figure out who this guy was and what it all meant. Thankfully, by now, I had some great role models around me who showed me what it looked like to live out a ministry calling. So, I thought about it often but wasn't quite sure what to do next.

Not long after that, my pastor got up to preach. We had a whole squad of maybe 20 young urban dudes just soaking in the Word and engaging in fellowship. Everything was clicking, and the worship experience was off the charts. The pastor was on fire, and during his sermon, he said, "Don't sit here and wait for me to die before you get your chance to minister! I'm not going anywhere anytime soon, so you need to get up and find your own pulpit!"

I don't know what everyone else heard, but to me, it was like he was saying, "Activate that call!"—the same call that the other dude had dropped on me earlier. I still wasn't sure what that meant, but it stirred something inside me.

Soon after that, my friend Dave invited me to go with him to a homeless shelter in downtown Detroit. He was like, "Let's go do some ministry there!" We were both in our 20s, trying to figure out life, marriage, kids, and now a ministry... I guess. So, off we went.

Man, it was crazy down there! People were screaming, glass was breaking, and it felt like we were stepping into a movie scene. We brought a couple of guys to keep things safe while we were doing our thing. We prayed for people, laid hands on them, and saw some unbelievable stuff happen—like people getting healed, just like in the Book of Acts.

At some point during all that madness, it finally clicked for me. I embraced my calling to be a pastor. Before that, I was all about tech stuff, marketing, and business planning, but deep down, I knew I was meant to pastor. It was like a light bulb went off in my head.

Sometimes, you just gotta dive into the chaos and take a leap of faith. Before all this, I'd tried kids' ministry, driven the church bus, and even led men's Bible study. Being in the thick of it helped me figure out what I was really called to do. You gotta step out first and have faith. Then, you'll start to hear what God is saying about your calling. And that's exactly what I did!

Embracing that second calling was one of the most unexpected and transformative experiences of my life. To be honest, I wasn't looking for it. I didn't feel like I was "pastor material" by any stretch of the imagination. But sometimes, God doesn't wait for you to feel ready. He just calls, and it's up to you to respond, even when you don't think you're capable or prepared.

After that homeless shelter experience in downtown Detroit, something shifted in me. I saw firsthand how ministry wasn't just about standing in front of a congregation in a suit, preaching from the pulpit. It was about being in the trenches, meeting people where they were, and letting God work through me to help them. That night at the shelter, I felt like I had found my pulpit—not the traditional kind, but the kind that mattered most: the streets, the people, and the real-life situations where God's presence was needed the most.

I'll be honest: I didn't have a plan for what was coming next. I had no formal seminary training or any clue on how to lead a church, and I was still getting comfortable just speaking in front of people. But like I said before, sometimes you just have to take a leap of faith. You might not have all the answers, but you move forward, trusting that God will fill in the gaps. That's exactly what happened to me.

Soon after, I started getting more involved in church leadership. I found myself stepping up to take on roles I never imagined myself in. At first, it was small things— leading prayer meetings, organizing community outreach, and working with the youth. But each step was another layer of preparation for what was coming. The Lord was slowly building me up, teaching me, and showing me how to shepherd His people.

What I learned through this process is that the Lord doesn't always call the qualified. More often than not, He qualifies the called. I wasn't the smartest, the best speaker, or the most charismatic leader. But I had a heart for people, and I had a desire to serve. That was enough for God to work with. He took my willingness and turned it into something far greater than I could have ever done on my own.

Over time, I started preaching more regularly. I remember the first few sermons—my hands were shaking, my voice was trembling, and I wasn't sure if I was even making sense. But as I kept showing up and letting the Lord use me, I got better.

Looking back, it's amazing how far Jesus has brought me from that random moment when that preacher pointed me out and declared that I was called to be a pastor. I didn't see it then, but now I understand that He was planting a seed. It took time, patience, and a lot of trust, but that seed eventually grew into something I never could have imagined.

So, if you ever feel the Lord is calling you—whether it's to ministry, to help others, or to step into a new role you feel unprepared for—don't let fear or self-doubt hold you back. Just take that first step, even if it feels small and uncertain. He will guide you the rest of the way, and I promise it will be worth it.

A CALL OF A LIFESTYLE

We all have a call we need to answer. God didn't just create us to exist just for existing sake. He created us to serve him, and while mine was urban ministry, yours might be different. It could be teaching, leading, singing, etc. The most important thing is to discover your call and answer it.

When the Lord created man, he deposited a lot of resources in us. These resources aren't just for decoration or fashion but to serve Him in his grand plan for humanity.

When we take the time to reflect on what He has placed inside of us, we begin to see that our gifts, talents, and passions are meant for something far greater than ourselves. They are the tools the Lord has given us to contribute to His purpose on Earth. Each of us has a unique calling, and it's up to us to seek out what that calling is and to follow it faithfully.

It's easy to get caught up in our hustle and forget that we are here for more than just going through the motions. We have a higher purpose. Whether your calling involves preaching, teaching, caregiving, or even something as simple as offering a listening ear to someone in need, it's all part of God's greater plan. No role is too small or insignificant in His eyes. Sometimes, we think we need to have some grand, visible role to make an impact, but that's not always the case. Often, it's the little things that make the biggest difference. Like doing life with someone, checking up on members of your church, etc.

One thing I've learned in my own journey is that discovering your calling doesn't happen overnight. It requires patience, prayer, and sometimes, a bit of trial and error. There will be moments of doubt, times when you question whether you're really on the right path. But those moments are part of the process, and they help refine and shape you for the work He has prepared for you. The important thing is not to give up when things get tough.

It's also important to remember that our calling isn't static. It can evolve and change over time as we grow and mature in our faith. What God calls you to today might look different a few years from now, just like my call also changed over time. You will see that in the next subtopic. That's why it's so important to remain open and attentive to the Lord's leadings. We need to be flexible and willing to adjust and adapt as God reveals new opportunities and directions for us.

What matters most is that we live with intentionality and a heart committed to serving God in whatever way He leads us. But Jesus doesn't call us to do things in our own strength. He equips us with everything we need to fulfill the purpose He has for our lives. He called me into urban ministry and equipped me with everything I needed for the ministry. He didn't fail me in my calling; He won't fail you in yours. Let me share the story of my calling with you.

After relocating from Detroit back to Grand Rapids—a journey of two and a half hours—I felt compelled to create something meaningful in the same community where I grew up. I was a successful man in the tech industry, and I am doing amazing work for Jesus. However, long-term clarity was needed.

Initially, our church was affiliated with a denomination, but as time progressed, we made the decision to become non-denominational. We invested our efforts into running youth ministries, mentoring children in public schools, and even offering martial arts classes. We sought to engage young people, sharing the love of Christ in relevant ways. However, despite our dedication, the church did not grow as I had anticipated.

"If you are called to the ministry, you aren't promised an easy life, but you are promised a life that's worthwhile"

~Kieth Drury~

I found myself grappling with questions. Was the church failing? Were we missing something crucial? Reflecting on those times, I now understand that our metrics were misaligned. We had become preoccupied with attendance, focusing on how many individuals filled the seats—when we should have celebrated the lives we were positively impacting and people being made whole. We were embodying the principles found in James 2:14-17, demonstrating faith through action, even if our efforts did not align with traditional notions of church success.

As time went on, some of the talented individuals who had joined our community felt called to pursue other ministry opportunities. This was disheartening, yet it was always our mission to bring them in, sit them down, raise them up, and send them out. I was already bearing a heavy burden, and when a young man who was like a nephew to me named Snooter was brutally murdered, it felt as though the ground beneath me had crumbled. That event was the tipping point, the culmination of an already overwhelming grief. It struck far too close to home, and I felt powerless and frustrated with the limitations of an organized church.

Consequently, my family and I decided to hold worship services at home. This arrangement provided a more intimate and personal way to seek God together. However, once again, that wife that the Lord gave me felt a calling to return to a more traditional church

Eventually, I accompanied her to a different church, unaware that it was known for sending out congregants to establish new ministries. It was a vibrant and healthy community, and as I began to heal, my mentor, Henry Balma, invited me to a conference in Azusa, California. This invitation proved transformative.

During the conference, a speaker named Larry posed a thought-provoking question: "What if God has called you to do urban ministry for the rest of your life?" That question resonated deeply within me. My wife and I exchanged knowing glances, tears flowing as we both recognized the profound tug on our hearts regarding our next steps.

Together, we approached the altar, much like we had done in the past, but this time, the commitment felt renewed. We were resubmitting our lives to urban ministry for the long term. It was a significant moment, representing a fresh start and a new chapter in our lives. We embraced the call of a lifetime—urban ministry.

Today, I stand ready to engage in this journey, equipped with the lessons learned from my past and filled with hope for the future. Ultimately, it is not merely about running a church; it is about making a meaningful difference in the lives of individuals, one heart at a time. This mission is what drives me forward.

So, wherever you are in life, I encourage you to seek out what God has placed inside you. Don't be afraid to step into your calling, knowing that God will walk with you every step of the way. He created you with a purpose in mind, and when you answer that call, you will find the true fulfillment that only comes from living out His plan for your life.

CALL TO TRANSITION

Life is full of transitions, some planned and some unexpected, but each one has its own purpose. Whether in work, relationships, or personal growth, we are often called to move forward, to step into something new. And while transitions can be unsettling, they are also essential to our growth, development, and fulfillment of our purpose. When we feel that nudge—a sense that it's time to shift gears—it's important to recognize that this is often a divine call to a new season of life. Transition is not about abandoning what you've built; it's about embracing what's next.

Change is one of those things that can sneak up on us. We often resist it, especially when we're comfortable or settled in a certain routine. But comfort can sometimes hold us back from our true potential. In life, we tend to hold onto what's familiar, even when we feel that tug in our hearts to step out into something different. We are used to holding onto what we are used to and oftentimes don't want to challenge ourselves to take new steps. This hesitation can come from fear, uncertainty, or simply the weight of responsibilities that we've accumulated over time. However, the call to transition is about trusting that there's more ahead—something greater that we may not yet see clearly.

The journey of transition often starts with a sense of dissatisfaction or a feeling that what worked before is no longer aligning with where we are. We might try to ignore it, rationalize it, or push it aside. But deep down, we know when it's time to move. It's like when a season changes in nature—you can feel it in the air before you see the leaves fall. In the same way, we can feel it when a transition is on the horizon in our lives.

One of the most critical parts of navigating a transition is self-awareness. You must be honest with yourself about where you are and where you believe you're being called to go. That kind of reflection doesn't come easily in the middle of a busy life. It takes intentional time, a pause to reflect, and the courage to ask the hard questions. Am I still passionate about what I'm doing? Is this the best use of my talents? Is there something else I feel drawn to? The answers to these questions often reveal the next steps, even when we don't have a complete understanding of what is ahead.

It's also important to recognize that transitions are rarely just about us. They often involve other people—those we lead, work with, or care for. When we feel the call to transition, it impacts the people around us. And that's part of what makes these decisions so challenging. Letting go of a role, a position, or even a relationship can feel like we're letting others down. But in truth, when we stay too long in a place where we're no longer growing, we can limit the growth of those around us, too. Stepping out of the way often creates space for others to rise, take on new responsibilities, and lead in ways they couldn't before.

Transition doesn't mean failure. It doesn't mean you didn't do your job or fulfill your calling. It means you've done what you were meant to do for that season, and now it's time for someone else to step in. Sometimes, our greatest act of leadership is knowing when to let go and pass the baton. This process of handing things over, while bittersweet, is a crucial part of growth for both ourselves and those we leave behind. In many cases, our departure creates opportunities for others to shine in ways they never would have while we were still in the spotlight.

The fear of transition often comes from the unknown. We worry about what's next, whether we'll succeed, or if we're even making the right choice. But transition is not the end; it's simply the beginning of a new chapter. And while the future may be uncertain, it's important to trust the process. There's peace in knowing that life's transitions are often orchestrated for our benefit, even when they seem disruptive at first. It's about stepping into that unknown with faith, trusting that what lies ahead is part of a bigger plan.

One of the things that can help during a transition is having a solid support system. Whether it's a mentor, family, or close friends, having people you can talk to and lean on during times of change makes all the difference. These are the people who remind you of your strengths when you doubt yourself and help you see the bigger picture when you're caught up in the details. Surrounding yourself with those who understand your vision and support your growth can help ease the anxiety that often comes with transitions.

It's also important to understand that transitions are not always immediate. Sometimes, the call to transition comes long before the actual shift happens. There may be a period of preparation where you're still in your current role but getting ready for what's next. This can be a time of reflection, learning, and gathering the resources you need for the new chapter. Transition is a process, not a single moment.

One amazing thing about transition is that things may not go according to your plan, and that's okay. Often, we discover new opportunities along the way—things we didn't anticipate when we first felt the call to move on. Being open to these surprises is part of the beauty of transition. It allows us to grow in unexpected ways and step into roles we never would have considered before.

Like I always say, the call to transition is about growth. It's about

I was pastoring at the Edge Church in Grand Rapids, right in the heart of the vibrant hip-hop culture. Imagine a lively, multi-ethnic, multi-generational church where youth and young adults feel welcomed and loved. We're not just filling seats; we're raising people up spiritually and sending them out to share the good news of Christ. It's like living out the Great Commission from Matthew 28:19-20 but in our own unique, urban way.

But then, around year nine or ten, I felt this strong pull—a sense that God was nudging me to move on. I had poured so much into the lives of young people, and I could see several of them stepping into leadership roles. I remember having a heart-to-heart with one of my sons from the Church Beacon Light, a gifted speaker and artist. I asked him if he'd consider taking over the church. He was fantastic—people loved him, and he truly understood our culture. But then he said something that struck me deeply. He told me, "We don't need another pastor who's always on the go like you and me. We need someone who can be stable, a shepherd who's here with the people." Ouch! That hit me right in the gut.

That conversation made me stop and think. I told myself, "Alright, I need to be that shepherding pastor." But to be honest, that didn't go as smoothly as I hoped. I leaned on other capable people to take on that shepherding role, and they did a wonderful job, but I was still hanging around, caught up in my own hesitation. Urban ministry

Here I was, the guy who jumps on planes to spread the Gospel in places it's never been, yet I was stuck when it came to leaving. I even had this strange experience at a church dedication. I stepped into the restroom, and while I was there, a man walked in and started chatting with me. Now, if you're a guy, you know that bathroom time is sacred and meant for silence! But this guy, out of nowhere, started telling me how he felt called to leave his church to help others. I was taken aback and thought, "Is this guy an angel or something?"

Honestly, I didn't remember much about the service after that. I was wrestling with what he had said. Later, as my wife and I sat in the car, I turned to her and asked, "When do you think I'm done?" She had pretty much reached her limit with my back-and-forth about quitting, but finally, she said, "I think you're done in January."

That was my wake-up call. We drove to meet with Kirt and Tisa, our assistant and outreach pastors. I laid it all out for Kirt, saying, "I'm done. I'm handing this over to you." And you know what? They both felt a calling to step up. It became clear that if I hadn't finally decided to be obedient, they wouldn't have felt empowered to take the lead. It reminded me of the story of David and Saul—Saul was still acting like king long after God had anointed David, and I realized it was time for me to let go.

Today, Kirt, the dude I mentored for eight years, is now the lead pastor of that church. It wasn't an easy transition, seeing that the founding Pastor was stepping away; there were challenges and frustrations along the way. But stepping down was essential for both of us. It wasn't about abandoning my ministry or my calling; it was about embracing a new chapter and getting out of the way, allowing a young leader to stretch out and lead. My commitment to urban ministry remained as strong as ever, and God started opening new doors for me. Now, I find myself in a new role where I pastor pastors across the U.S. and beyond through the Nitrogen Urban Network. My heart is still dedicated to serving the urban community, and I'm fully committed to this mission for the long haul. You can reach out to us on our website: **www.nitrogennetwork.org** to join this movement.

Just like Paul said in 1 Corinthians 9:24-27, I'm running this race with purpose, determined to make a lasting impact in the lives of those around me.

Through the ever-challenging and changing storm called life, we were created by the master creator. This means that we have a Creator who knows exactly how we are wired and what we're meant and designed to do. He holds the playbook, the blueprint, and the manual, which outline how we are intended to move in this world. We know it's him when we're naturally gifted at something, and it ultimately brings glory to God.

As I always say, transitions are never easy, but they are necessary. As I stepped down from leading The Edge Church, I realized that my journey wasn't ending; it was shifting into something new, something I hadn't yet fully understood. It wasn't just about moving on but about making space for the next generation to take the lead and grow in their callings. I had to let go so that others could rise.

As Kirt took over, I saw firsthand how important it was to trust in God's timing, even when it didn't make sense to me. There were challenges, yes, but there was also peace. I had spent years mentoring and pouring into the lives of young leaders, and now it was their time to step up and carry the mantle. I had been clinging to my role because of my own insecurities and fears about what was next. But once I let go, Jesus revealed new opportunities I couldn't have imagined before.

In handing over the reins, I learned something crucial about leadership: sometimes, the greatest act of leadership is knowing when to step aside. It's about realizing that our role isn't always to stay in one place forever but to prepare the way for others to step in and lead. By doing so, we allow the community to grow, evolve, and thrive in ways that wouldn't be possible if we stayed too long.

Stepping down was also an act of faith. I didn't know what would come next for me, but I trusted that God had a plan. And He did.

The transition opened doors for me to serve in new ways, ways that aligned with my passion for urban ministry but on a larger scale. Now, as part of the Nitrogen Urban Network, I mentor and guide pastors across the U.S. and beyond, helping them navigate their own challenges in urban ministry. It's a role that allows me to continue serving the communities I love while also helping others find their place in this work.

I've come to understand that the Lord knows exactly how we are wired and what we are meant to do. He created us with specific gifts and talents, and when we align with His plan, we find fulfillment in ways we never could on our own. This journey has taught me to lean into my strengths and trust in the gifts God has given me. When we use those gifts to serve others, we not only find our purpose, but we bring glory to the Lord in the process.

As I reflect on this transition, I see how each step, each decision, was part of a greater plan. The process wasn't always clear, but I learned to trust that the Lord had already written the blueprint for my life. And that's the beauty of it all—when we let go of our own need to control, we allow Jesus to take the lead, and that's when amazing things start to happen.

Life Application: Every person on this planet has a unique calling in their life. God has crafted each of us with a specific purpose, something special we're meant to do in His name and for His glory. Sometimes, it takes a while to figure that out. It all starts with surrender and continuing to seek Him. I mean, really seeking Him with all you got!!! Start asking yourself some honest questions. What are those things that come naturally to you? What activities make time fly by because you're so engrossed in them? Reflecting on your gifts and talents is crucial.

REFLECTION QUESTIONS

- What experiences, both positive and negative, have shaped your understanding of your calling? How have they prepared you for the work God has for you?

- In what ways have you struggled with feelings of inadequacy or unworthiness when it comes to fulfilling your calling? How can you learn to embrace God's power and provision in the midst of your weaknesses?

- Who are the people in your life who have spoken into your calling or encouraged you to step out in faith? How can you cultivate more of those types of relationships?

- What specific steps do you feel God is calling you to take in order to move forward in your purpose? What fears or doubts are holding you back from obedience?

- How can you begin to actively seek God's will for your life on a daily basis rather than waiting for a dramatic "burning bush" moment? What habits or practices can you implement to stay attuned to His leading?

CALL TO ACTION

Take some time to prayerfully reflect on your calling. Ask God to reveal areas where you may be resisting or doubting His plan for your life. Make a commitment to surrender your insecurities and trust that He will equip you for the task at hand. Seek out mentors or community groups that can provide encouragement and accountability as you step out in faith.

Chapter Two
OCCUPATION

"Work is good, and it's a gift from God."

From the time we're young, there's always that exciting question people love to ask, *"What do you want to be when you grow up?"* It's a question that sparks our imagi -nation and gets us thinking about the future in a way that's full of possibility. As kids, we dream big, with answers like astronauts, doctors, or even superheroes. It's a fun way to envision what our future might look like, and there's no limit to where our minds can take us.

As we grow older, that question starts to shift. By the time we're in our twenties, it changes from *"What do you want to be?"'* to*"What do you do for a living?"* While it might seem like the shift is from dream to reality, the truth is that it's still about the same thing: *figuring out what we contribute to the world and how we spend our days.*

There's something fulfilling about being able to answer that question with pride, knowing that you've found your place in the world of occupation. Whether you're a teacher, doctor, accountant, real estate agent, or even an Instagram influencer (yes, that's a thing now!), what you do for a living is a big part of your identity, and for good reason.

Our occupation is more than just a way to make money. It's a way to make an impact, to contribute to society, and to shape our daily lives in great ways. The word "occupation" carries a great purpose. It's not just about the paycheck but about the role you play in the bigger picture. When you think about it, your occupation is the way you use your skills, talents, and abilities to make the world around you a better place. It's the way you add value to the lives of others, whether it's by educating students, healing patients, solving financial problems, helping people find their dream homes, or entertaining and influencing others online.

For many people, their occupation gives them pride and fulfillment. It's not just the thing they do to pay the bills; it's something they enjoy, something that challenges them and allows them to grow. Think about the feeling you get when you've accomplished something at work – whether it's completing a big project, helping a client, or hitting a personal goal. That sense of achievement is a big part of why people find meaning in their jobs. It's more than just clocking in and out; it's about making progress, learning new things, and striving to do better every day.

Some people are fortunate enough to find an occupation that aligns perfectly with their passion. For them, work doesn't feel like a chore – it feels like a calling. They wake up excited to get to work because they know they're doing something they love. Whether they're teaching, designing, creating, or building, their occupation is a reflection of their interests and values. When you find work that you're passionate about, it's not just a job; it's an extension of who you are. It's a way to express yourself and share your gifts with the world. And there's something incredibly rewarding about that.

Even for those whose jobs may not be their ultimate dream, there's still something valuable about the work they do. Every occupation, no matter what it is, plays an important role in the functioning of our society. From the person who delivers your mail to the person who helps you at the grocery store, every job matters.

Beyond the essential services that jobs provide, there's something to be said about the discipline and structure that come from having an occupation. Work gives us routine, stability, and a sense of responsibility. It's a way to contribute and build the life we want to live.

In today's world, the concept of an occupation has become more flexible than ever. People aren't tied to just one job or one career path for their entire lives. Instead, we're seeing more variety in the way people work. Some people switch careers several times, while others create side hustles or freelance on the side. There are so many ways to make a living, and that means there are more opportunities than ever to find work that feels meaningful and exciting. Whether you're working a traditional 9-to-5, running your own business, or balancing multiple gigs, there's something empowering about being in control of your career and designing it in a way that fits your life.

In the digital age, we're also seeing new kinds of occupations emerge, from social media influencers to content creators to remote workers who can do their jobs from anywhere in the world. The idea of what work looks like is constantly evolving, and that's an exciting thing. It means that there are more possibilities than ever to find a career path that suits your unique skills and interests. Whether you're working from a laptop in a coffee shop or leading a team in an office, your occupation is a reflection of the world we live in today – dynamic, flexible, and full of potential.

Above all, I want you to know that your occupation is an important part of who you are, but it's not the only part. It's one of the many ways you can contribute to the world and express your talents, but it doesn't define you completely. The great thing about work is that it can be a tool to help you achieve your goals, whether those goals are professional, personal, or a combination of both. For some, that means climbing the corporate ladder and achieving success in their field. For others, it means finding the balance between work and life so they can spend more time with family or pursue hobbies and passions outside of their job.

At the end of the day, your occupation is something you should be proud of, no matter what it is. It's the way you show up in the world, the way you contribute, and the way you make a difference. Whether you're just starting out in your career or have been in the workforce for decades, there's always room to grow, learn, and find new opportunities. So the next time someone asks, "What do you do for a living?" answer with pride, knowing that your occupation is not just about making money – it is part of your purpose on earth.

Your job, your career, and your occupation are all part of your purpose, and they are things you must deliberate about.

WORK IS GOOD

If you take a step back and look at history, people had a different relationship with work back in the day. I'm a huge fan of documentaries, especially ones that take a deep dive into our past, like *The Men That Made America*. If you're anything like me, you can binge-watch these kinds of shows for hours! This is a docu-series that was released on the History Channel in 2012. It focuses on some of the most influential dudes in American history, specifically during the late 1800s and early 1900s. It highlights John D. Rockefeller, Andrew Carnegie, J.P. Morgan, and Cornelius Vanderbilt, who played major roles in shaping the economy and society of the United States.

The series explores their personal stories, showing how their ambition, innovation, and oftentimes foul business practices played a part in their success. Through a mix of dramatic reenactments, interviews with historians, and old-school footage, the show provides a look at how their philosophies and practices not only built their fortunes but also transformed America into a global economic beast. It's a crazy exploration of ambition, power, and the complex legacies left behind by these influential figures. Through it all, one of the common values these pioneers shared was their work ethic. In order to accomplish what was impossible, they had to believe in the foundational principle of hard work.

Now, let's fast-forward to our current reality. Technology has completely transformed the landscape of work. As an IT engineer, I was right in the thick of it during the tech boom of the late '90s and early 2000s, and let me tell you, it was a wild ride! Similar to today, it seemed like every week, something new was released. We used to say, "From the store to the door." This means that once it leaves the store and gets to your door, it's old. This is now multiplied by 100 with the recent advancement of AI. Tasks that used to take days could now be completed in just a few hours, and things that once took hours can now be done in minutes. It's incredible how far we've come!

But here's the thing, though, while technology has made our lives easier and more efficient, it has also shifted the expectations about work for many. Everything is fast-paced. It's all about getting things done as quickly as possible, which naturally leads to taking the road of least resistance. Oftentimes, lacking the grit that revolutionizes a society. I think Eric Thomas (ET), one of the leading motivational speakers of our time, would say, "We have lost that dog you need to succeed." This new technology boom has slowly shaped the perspective of work in people's minds forever. There was a time when hard work was honorable and desired. The emotional tie to work looked different. You just did what you had to do. The drive to do this was the commitment to the responsibility of taking care of yourself and those you love.

WARNING: I'm about to sound like an old crazy man. Nowadays, there's this overwhelming pressure to have a deep passion or *love* for what you do. It's as if society has placed an expectation on us that things should be fast and easy and that our jobs should be a love story with violins playing in the background.

Social media influencers often tell the world, "Find your passion and go for it!" But let's be real for a moment: how many of the greats I mentioned earlier were "in love" with their first jobs? For the most part, they had to work their way up and do what they had to do. They were not necessarily driven because they were passionate about their current jobs but because they had to make a living and build something for the future.

Today, it seems like people feel they can hop from job to job, always searching for the next big thing that will fulfill them. It's become the norm to leave a job every year or two in hopes of finding something more exciting or fulfilling. While I think it's great to seek fulfillment in your work, this constant chase can lead to an unquenchable thirst for satisfaction that only God can truly fulfill. No job, no career, and no business can ultimately bring us the contentment we crave.

I'm not suggesting we roll the clock back and kill technology. I am that person that uses AI in my everyday life. But I see it as a tool that will assist in making me more efficient. I'm just saying we need to adjust our perspective on work. Instead of constantly asking ourselves, "How much do I love what I do?" What if we shifted our focus to gratitude? What if we started appreciating the work in front of us for what it is?

Think about this: the God of the universe, who could easily crush us if He wanted to, has given us an amazing world to live in and the responsibility to take care of it. In Genesis, He created us to work and steward the earth. Work is a part of our purpose! It's a gift, not a curse.

Now, I know what you might be thinking: "But work can be tough! It can be stressful!" And you're absolutely right. After the fall, there's no denying that work became harder. Genesis 3:19 tells us we'll have to work by the sweat of our brow. But let's not forget that God gave humanity work to do before the fall. Adam was given the responsibility of naming the animals and taking care of the garden before sin came into the scene. Those were jobs given to him by God. And that work was meaningful, God-honoring, and straight-up good.

So, if you're imagining paradise as a hammock on the beach with no responsibilities, think again! Adam had his own version of 9 to 5, except it probably involved fewer emails and definitely less paperwork.

What does this tell us? Work was always part of the Lord's plan for humanity. The idea was for humans to partner with God in taking care of the earth. In other words, work is actually a good thing. It's a blessing! Okay, maybe not the kind of blessing you pray for on a Sunday morning, but it's a gift nonetheless. And we were created to work.

WORK BY DESIGN

When we recognize that work is a part of God's design, we can appreciate it for what it is. In seeking work to care for this place He gave us, called Earth, we can see His master plan laid out—a plan to give us hope and a future, a plan to fulfill our unique God-given purpose. And yes, there may come a time when your calling and your job align perfectly, where you get to do what you're passionate about and get paid for it. That's the dream for many, and that's great. But now it's like becoming a top 3 NBA draft pick—it's rare, and not everyone will have that opportunity, and that's perfectly okay!

If you know what you're called to do and you're working in a job that provides for your family, supports your community, and allows you to give to your local church, then you're on the right track. You are handling your business, and trust me, God is pleased with that. It's not always about chasing after passion; it's about being faithful in the work you have, and passion will naturally find you. Pursue that job with dedication, and I promise you'll find joy in the process. As Colossians 3:23 reminds us, "Whatever you do, work heartily, as for the Lord and not for men."

When we shift our priority from seeking our own satisfaction to fulfilling our God-given purpose through work, that's when we truly start to find pleasure in the work He has allowed us to do. So, whether you're in a corporate office, teaching in a classroom, or working in a trade, remember that your work matters. It's not just about earning a paycheck; it's a way to honor God, serve others, and make a difference in the world. Embrace it, and you just might find the fulfillment you've been looking for.

When you start to view your work as more than just a means to earn a paycheck, something inside shifts, you realize that your job, no matter what it is, is part of the bigger picture. It's not just about you or your personal satisfaction; it's about serving others and glorifying God in the process. This perspective changes the way you approach your day-to-day tasks. Whether you're filing paperwork, managing a team, teaching a classroom full of students, or working with your hands in a trade, you begin to understand that every role you play matters.

In today's world, it can be easy to get caught up in comparing yourself to others, especially when it comes to careers. We live in an age of social media, where it seems like everyone else is thriving in their "dream job" or chasing after their passions. We see influencers traveling the world, people launching successful businesses, or others reaching the top of their professions. It can make you feel like maybe what you're doing isn't good enough. But that's not the truth. The truth is that the Lord has given each of us a unique path, and it won't look the same for everyone.

For some people, their careers might align perfectly with their passions, and that's wonderful. However, for others, their job might be more about fulfilling responsibilities, providing for their family, and supporting their community. And that's equally important. There's a lot of honor in showing up every day and doing the work that needs to be done, even when it doesn't feel glamorous or exciting. Every job has value, and every effort matters, no matter how small it may seem.

This is where the idea of faithfulness comes in. Being faithful in your work means committing to doing your best, even when the work feels mundane or challenging. It means being trustworthy, reliable, and consistent. And in doing so, you're building something far more valuable than just a career—you're building character. When you take pride in your work and do it to the best of your ability, even when no one's watching, you are honoring God. You are using the gifts He has given you in a way that reflects His goodness.

It's important to remember that work doesn't always have to be driven by passion. Passion is a great motivator, but it isn't the only thing that gives work meaning. Some of the most fulfilling jobs don't

Take a moment to think about the people in your life whose jobs might not be considered "dream" jobs by society's standards but who find great fulfillment in what they do. Maybe it's the nurse who works long hours but takes pride in caring for patients or the teacher who stays late to help a struggling student. Maybe it's the mechanic who loves the satisfaction of fixing a car or the small business owner who takes joy in serving their community. These people have found meaning in their work not because it's flashy or because it brings them fame but because they see the difference they're making in the lives of others.

Work also has a ripple effect. When you show up every day and do your job with dedication, it impacts the people around you—your coworkers, customers, clients, and even your family. Your work is a reflection of who you are, and when you do it well, it encourages others to do the same. In this way, work becomes a form of service. You are serving not just yourself but the people who benefit from your efforts, and that's a powerful thing.

There's this fulfillment that comes from knowing you are doing your work perfectly. Even when it feels like no one is noticing, Jesus sees. He knows your heart, and He knows the effort you're putting in. He sees the sacrifices you make to provide for your family, to support your community, and to contribute to the world around you. And He is pleased with that.

Scripture often talks about the importance of work, but it also emphasizes rest. It's important to find a balance between working hard and resting well. God created the Sabbath as a day of rest, a time to rest, recharge, and refocus. In today's fast-paced world, we often feel the pressure to constantly do something and be productive at all times. But rest is just as important as work. It allows us to take a step back, reflect, and reconnect with God. When we rest, we are reminded that our worth isn't tied to how much we accomplish or how hard we work. Our worth comes from being children of God.

When you think about your work from this perspective, it takes some of the pressure off. You don't have to strive for perfection or constantly push yourself to achieve more. Instead, you can focus on being faithful in the work you've been given and trusting that the Lord will guide you through it. Whether you're in a season where you love your job or in a season where work feels like a challenge, know that God is with you in both. He's not only interested in the big moments of success but also in the small, everyday moments of faithfulness.

As you continue to work, keep your eyes open for opportunities to serve others. Look for ways to be a blessing to those around you. Sometimes, the greatest joy in work comes not from what we achieve but from the ways we help others along the way. Maybe it's a kind word to a coworker who's having a tough day or going the extra mile to make sure a customer is satisfied. This small kindness can make a big difference and bring purpose to your work that goes beyond the job itself.

Above all, work is a gift. It's a chance to use the talents and abilities God has given you to make a positive impact on the world. Whether your job is exactly what you dreamed of or it's something you're still growing into, know that your work has value. Embrace it, be faithful to it, and trust that God is using it—and you—for His greater purpose. And in doing so, you just might find that fulfillment you've been searching for all along.

RESPONDING TO WORKPLACE CHALLENGES

Work is an important part of our lives. It provides for our needs, helps us contribute to society, and allows us to use the skills God has given us. But as anyone who's ever had a job knows, the workplace isn't always easy. We face challenges, frustrations, and tough decisions that can make it hard to keep a positive attitude and maintain our values. Yet, as Christians, we must respond to these challenges in a way that reflects Jesus.

It's easy to have a good attitude when things are going well at work, but the true test of our character comes when we find ourselves in difficult environments. Maybe you work for a demanding boss who never seems satisfied, or maybe your workplace is filled with gossip and negativity. It can be tough to stay positive and maintain your integrity when everyone around you seems to be doing the opposite.

One way to handle situations like this is to be intentional about the way you respond to challenging situations. For example, if a coworker speaks to you harshly or unfairly criticizes your work, it can be tempting to respond in anger or defensiveness. Instead, you can choose to respond with grace and patience, reflecting Christ in the way you handle conflict. This doesn't mean letting people walk all over you, but it does mean responding in a way that honors God.

It's also important to guard your heart against the negativity that can sometimes dominate the workplace. If gossip, complaining, or cynicism are common among your coworkers, it's easy to get pulled into that mindset. Instead of joining in on the negativity, we can choose to focus on the positive and be a light in the darkness.

Another challenge you can face in your career maybe when you are faced with *an ethical dilemma*. It could be something small, like being asked to bend the rules to meet a deadline, or something more serious, like being pressured to act dishonestly for the sake of profit. In these moments, it can be difficult to know what to do, especially if you're worried about how it might affect your job or relationships with coworkers.

The first thing to remember when facing an ethical dilemma is to seek wisdom from the Lord. When you're unsure of what the right course of action is, take time to pray and ask Him for guidance. He knows the situation better than anyone, and He will provide the wisdom we need if we ask for it.

In addition to seeking wisdom from the Lord, it's also important to have the courage to stand up for what's right. It can be tempting to go along with something unethical if it seems like " everyone else is doing it" or if you're worried about losing your job. However, choosing integrity over convenience might not always be easy, but it is always the right thing to do.

One way to prepare yourself for these moments is to have clear personal values and boundaries before you're ever faced with a dilemma. Know where you stand on important issues, and decide ahead of time that you will not compromise your values, no matter the cost. This can help you feel more confident in your decision-making when tough situations arise because you won't be making choices out of fear or uncertainty but out of a commitment to live according to your faith.

If you find yourself in a situation where you need to speak up about something unethical, do so in a respectful and constructive manner. Be honest about your concerns, but do so in a way that is thoughtful and kind. You may need to have difficult conversations with your boss or coworkers, but approaching these conversations with humility and respect can help you maintain your integrity without burning bridges.

Another thing I want you to also understand is that workplaces are full of people with different personalities, backgrounds, and beliefs, which can sometimes lead to friction. You might have a coworker who is difficult to get along with, or maybe you work with people

One way to be gracious is by being patient and forgiving. People will inevitably make mistakes, and there will be times when coworkers frustrate or hurt you. Instead of holding onto grudges or letting bitterness take over you, choose to forgive and move on with a spirit of kindness.

Being gracious also means showing compassion to those who may be struggling. You never know what someone might be going through outside of work. A coworker who seems rude or distant may be dealing with personal challenges that you're unaware of. By showing empathy and offering a listening ear, you can create a positive and supportive work environment. You might even have the opportunity to share your faith with someone who is searching for hope.

Ministering to coworkers doesn't always mean preaching or sharing Bible verses (although there may be times when that's appropriate). Sometimes, the best way to minister to others is simply by living out your faith through your actions. When you consistently demonstrate kindness, integrity, and grace in the workplace, people will take notice. Your actions will speak of the love and grace of God, even if you never say a word about your faith.

There may also be moments when coworkers come to you for

advice or support. When this happens, take the opportunity to offer encouragement and point them toward God's truth. You don't have to have all the answers, but you can listen, pray for them, and remind them that they are not alone. In doing so, you are fulfilling the call to be a light in the world and to share the hope of Christ with those around you.

Responding to workplace challenges as a Christian isn't always easy, but it is possible when we rely on God for wisdom, strength, and grace. The workplace may present its share of challenges, but it is also a place where we have the opportunity to serve others, honor God, and make a positive impact. So the next time you face a tough situation at work, remember that you are not alone—God is with you, guiding you every step of the way.

ON TO THE NEXT

Life has a way of pushing us in new directions, and that's especially true when it comes to our careers. Whether you've been in the same job for years or you're just starting out, there comes a time when you might feel the need for something different, something more aligned with who you are and what you feel called to do. It's not always easy to know when to make that leap, but with discernment, faith, and trust in God's timing, you can navigate those transitions with confidence.

Let's talk about what it means to know when it's time to pursue a new vocational path, how to align job changes with your God-given calling, and, perhaps most importantly, how to trust God's provision during those uncertain transitions.

First off, how do you know when it's time for a change? This is a tough question, and there's no one-size-fits-all answer. Some people know right away when they've outgrown a job or when they're no longer in the right place. Others feel more uncertain, perhaps waiting for a clear sign or confirmation that it's time to move on.

One of the first indicators that it might be time for a new vocational path is the dissatisfaction or unrest that doesn't go away. You might find yourself feeling unfulfilled in your current role, not because the work is hard, but because it no longer excites or challenges you. You may feel like you're just going through the motions without any real sense of purpose or connection to what you're doing.

Sometimes, this feeling can be a gentle nudge from God, urging you to consider whether you're living out the calling He has for you. It's important to pause and ask yourself some key questions: "Is this job allowing me to use my gifts in a meaningful way?" "Am I growing spiritually, emotionally, and professionally in this role?" "Do I feel that I am where the Lord wants me to be right now?"

If the answer to these questions is consistently no, it might be time to prayerfully consider a change. But discerning whether to make a move also requires patience. Sometimes, we can mistake temporary discomfort for a sign that we need to quit, when really, Jesus may be calling us to stick it out a little longer for reasons we don't yet understand. This is why prayer and discernment are so important.

Another key indicator is when the doors to new opportunities start to open. Maybe you've been thinking about a career change for a while, but you weren't sure if it was the right time. Then, suddenly, you start getting calls for interviews, or you hear about job openings in a field you've been interested in. When Jesus opens doors, He often does so in ways that align with His timing, not necessarily ours.

Once you've discerned that it might be time to move on, the next step is to make sure that any new vocational path aligns with your God-given calling. This is crucial because it's easy to be tempted by higher salaries, better benefits, or more prestigious titles without considering whether the new role truly fits into God's plan for your life.

So, what does it mean to align your job with your calling? First, it means recognizing that your calling isn't just about what you're good at; it's about how you use your gifts to serve others and glorify Jesus. Your calling is the unique combination of skills, passions, and opportunities that the Lord has given you to make a difference in the world. It's not just about finding a job that you enjoy, or that pays well; it's about finding work that allows you to live out your faith in meaningful ways.

To align your career choices with your calling, start by reflecting on the gifts and talents that God has given you. What are you naturally good at? What are the things you do that bring you the most joy and fulfillment? These are often clues to what your calling might be.

Next, consider how these gifts can be used to serve others. Your vocation should be more than just a way to make a living—it should be a way to make an impact. Whether you're teaching, leading, creating, or serving in some other capacity, your work should be an expression of the love and care that Jesus has for the world.

And don't forget to seek counsel from those who know you well and understand your faith. Sometimes, others can see our strengths and gifts more clearly than we can. Talk to trusted friends, mentors, or spiritual advisors about your decision. They can provide valuable insight and help you stay focused on what matters most.

Be willing to trust that God may call you to something unexpected. Sometimes, the roles we're most drawn to don't seem to make sense on paper. Maybe they don't come with the pay or status we were hoping for, or maybe they involve stepping out of our comfort zone in a big way. But if you feel peace and purpose in a new direction, even if it's not what you expected, it may be worth taking the leap.

Of course, discerning a new path and aligning it with your calling are just the beginning. Once you've decided to make a move, you still have to trust that God will provide for you along the way. This is often the hardest part of any career transition—the waiting, the uncertainty, and the fear of the unknown. But it's also where faith comes in.

When you take a step of faith and pursue a new job or career, you're trusting that the Lord will meet your needs. And the truth is, He always does. It may not look the way you expected, and the timing may not be exactly what you planned, but God's provision is always enough.

One of the biggest challenges during career transitions is the fear of financial instability. Will I be able to support my family? What if I can't find a job right away? These are valid concerns, and it's natural to worry about them. But remember that the Lord is your ultimate provider, not your job. He knows what you need, and He will not abandon you in a time of transition.

It's important to trust in His timing, even when it feels like things are moving slower than you'd like. Sometimes, the waiting period between jobs can be an opportunity for growth and reflection. Use this time to draw closer to Jesus, seek His guidance, and prepare for the next season of your life.

One way to stay grounded during this time is to focus on what you can control. While you can't always control how quickly a new job opportunity comes along, you can control how you respond in the meantime. Be diligent in your job search, but also be open to what

Jesus might be teaching you during this period of waiting. Are there areas of your life where He's calling you to grow? Are there relationships He wants you to invest in during this time?

One important thing I want you to remember is that your worth is not tied to your job. It can be easy to feel discouraged or even question your value when you're in between jobs, but your identity is in who you are as a child of God, not in what you do for a living. Whether you're employed or unemployed, in a high-paying job or a low-paying one, you are loved and valued by God. And that's something that no job title can ever change.

I want you to trust that God's plan for your life is good. He has a purpose for every season, and that includes times of transition. Even when the path ahead seems unclear, He is leading you toward something good.

At the end of the day, career transitions are a part of life. Sometimes, they're smooth and easy, and other times, they're filled with uncertainty and doubt. But no matter what, we can trust that God is with us at every step of the journey.

So, if you're feeling called to something new, take heart. God is guiding you, and He has a plan for your life that is better than anything you could imagine. Trust in His timing, seek His will, and step forward in faith. You might just find that the journey ahead is more rewarding than you ever dreamed.

SPREAD THE LOVE

In every stage of our lives, we have the chance to make a difference—not just through our own actions but by how we influence and uplift those around us. Whether you're a professional or just starting out in your career, there's a powerful way to spread love: by mentoring and developing future leaders, creating opportunities for others to flourish, and leveraging your influence to support and guide those around you. These actions not only enrich the lives of others but also help build a stronger, more supportive community. Let's look at these three ways you can spread love to people around you.

Mentoring is one of the most impactful ways you can spread love in both your personal and professional life. It's about sharing your knowledge, experience, and wisdom with someone and helping them grow and succeed. Think of mentoring as being a guide—a person who can offer advice, encouragement, and a bit of wisdom based on your own experiences.

When you mentor someone, you're not just giving them a hand up; you're investing in their future. This investment can take many forms, from regular one-on-one meetings to being available for advice when needed. The key is to be genuinely interested in their development and to support them in their individual needs and goals.

Effective mentoring involves more than just providing answers; it's about asking the right questions to help the mentee think through their own solutions. It's about listening and offering feedback that helps them reflect on their strengths and areas for growth. Good mentors understand that their role is not to dictate but to guide, helping the mentee find their own path while offering insights and support.

One of the most rewarding aspects of mentoring is seeing someone grow and achieve their goals. When you help someone develop their skills and confidence, you're not only making a difference in their life but also in the lives of those they will go on to impact. Future leaders are often shaped by the mentors they had along the way, and your influence can be a crucial part of that process.

Mentoring also has its benefits for you as a mentor. It can be incredibly fulfilling to see someone you've guided reach their potential. It's a way to give back and share the knowledge you've gained over the years. Plus, mentoring can offer new perspectives and insights that can enrich your own professional and personal life.

Creating opportunities for others to flourish is another way to spread love and make a meaningful impact. This doesn't just mean giving people chances to advance in their careers; it also involves supporting their personal and professional growth in a way that helps them reach their full potential.

Think about the ways you can open doors for others. If you're in a position to offer a job, a promotion, or even a chance to take on a challenging project, consider how you can create opportunities for others. This might involve recommending someone for a role, providing them with resources or training, or even just giving them a chance to prove themselves in a new area.

Creating opportunities also means recognizing and nurturing talent in those around you. Pay attention to the people you work with or interact with regularly. Who stands out because of their potential? Who shows promise but might need a little extra support to reach their goals? When you identify these people and provide them with opportunities to shine, you're helping to build a successful community.

It's important to remember that creating opportunities isn't just about advancing someone's career; it's also about supporting their overall growth. This might mean offering mentorship, providing constructive feedback, or just being a cheerleader for their efforts.

When you invest in the development of others, you're helping them build confidence and skills that will serve them well in the future.

Creating opportunities is also about creating an environment where people feel valued and supported. When people know that they have the chance to grow and succeed, they're more likely to be engaged and motivated. This can lead to a positive and productive atmosphere where everyone feels they have the chance to contribute and make a difference.

Lastly, we will talk about Leveraging your influence to look out for others. This is about using your position, experience, and connections to support and uplift those around you. Everyone has some level of influence, whether it's through their role at work, their involvement in community groups, or their relationships with friends and family. Using this influence to look out for others can have a great impact.

Consider how you can use your influence to advocate for others. This might involve speaking up for someone who's being overlooked or underrepresented, recommending them for opportunities, or supporting their initiatives. Your voice can help shine a light on their talents and contributions, giving them the recognition they deserve.

Sometimes, leveraging your influence means being a source of encouragement and support during challenging times. Everyone faces difficulties and setbacks, and having someone who believes in them and offers a helping hand can make a huge difference. Be there for others when they need it most, and offer your support in ways that are meaningful to them.

In all these efforts, remember that spreading love is not just about big gestures. It's also about the small, everyday actions that show you care. Whether it's offering a kind word, providing encouragement, or just being there for someone, every bit of support helps to create a positive and inclusive environment.

So, as you go through your day, think about how you can spread the love. Consider the ways you can mentor, create opportunities, and leverage your influence to make a difference in the lives of those around you. Your actions, big or small, can have a great impact, helping to build a community where everyone has the chance to flourish and succeed.

When you spread love, you're not just making the world a better place; you're also enriching your own life. The connections you build, the lives you touch, and the positive changes you help create are all part of a rewarding journey that benefits everyone involved. So embrace the opportunity to make a difference, and watch as the love you spread comes back to you in ways you never imagined.

Life Application: Our occupations should serve to support and fund the pursuit of our God-given calling, not define our identity or purpose. We must be willing to make difficult decisions about our work in order to align it with the unique way God wants to use us. This may mean stepping out of a comfortable career path or even accepting a lower-paying job that better fits our calling.

love you spread comes back to you in ways you never imagined.

Life Application: Our occupations should serve to support and fund the pursuit of our God-given calling, not define our identity or purpose. We must be willing to make difficult decisions about our work in order to align it with the unique way God wants to use us. This may mean stepping out of a comfortable career path or even accepting a lower-paying job that better fits our calling.

REFLECTION QUESTIONS

- How has your job defined your identity or self-worth? How can you start viewing it as a way to serve your God-given purpose?

- When did you last feel your job aligned with God's calling? What made that connection possible?

- What tough choices might you need to make to ensure your job supports your purpose? Are you ready to trust God and take a step of faith?

- How can you bring more gratitude and effort to your current job, even if it's not ideal? What small actions can you take to honor God through your work?

- Who in your life can offer wisdom and guidance as you balance your calling with your career? How can you strengthen those relationships?

CALL TO ACTION

Prayerfully examine your current occupation. Make a list of the pros and cons, and ask God to reveal any changes He might be leading you to make while you are in the place Where you are. If he leads, Be open to taking a step of faith, even if it means leaving a comfortable job or pursuing a new path. Trust that God will provide for you as you seek to honor Him through your work.

1. Create a budget based on the life you would like to live
2. Create a list of your top five skills and talents.
3. Reach out to friends, family, or colleagues for feedback on what they see as your strengths.
4. Explore Market Opportunities that align with your skills and the compensation you desire
5. Create a plan to go after it!
6. Choose one small action to take this week that moves you closer to your career or business goals.
7. Commit to being consistent in your actions, no matter how small.

Chapter Three
PASSION

Y ou've probably heard it a million times: "Find your passion!" It's the go-to advice for careers, life goals, and even those motivational posters plastered on walls. But what does it really mean to have passion for something? More importantly, how do you find it, and once you do, how do you keep that fire burning without it fizzing out like a dud firecracker?

"What excites you? What brings you joy?"

Spoiler alert: Passion isn't just about that rush of excitement when you start something new. It's about finding a purpose that makes you feel alive, a drive that pushes you forward—whether in your career, hobbies, or just the way you live day-to-day. Passion makes life feel more like an adventure and less like a list of to-do's. If you're ready to get fired up about your life, let's move into what it means to live with passion, how to find it, and how to keep it alive.

First of all, passion isn't some mysterious force reserved only for professional athletes, artists, or that one friend who seems to always have a new ultra-marathon on the horizon. It's something you can develop in your own life. Passion is that deep enthusiasm, love, and commitment to something that lights you up inside. It's that thing that makes hours fly by and leaves you feeling more energized than tired at the end of the day.

Passion doesn't always come naturally. Sometimes, you have to deliberately seek it out and develop it. Don't worry, though—it's not hiding somewhere under your couch. It's often right in front of you, waiting to be discovered.

One of the best ways to find your passion is to follow your curiosity. What are the things you naturally gravitate toward? Do you love cooking, writing, solving problems, or working with your hands? Your passions are often hidden in the things that spark your curiosity.

And if you're not sure what that is yet, try different stuff, even if you're terrible at it. Some of the greatest passions are discovered by accident. Maybe you've always wanted to try painting, but you're convinced you're not "artsy." Give it a go anyway! You might just stumble upon something that lights you up. Passion often follows persistence, so don't shy away from activities just because you're not an expert on day one.

While you're at it, take a minute to reflect on what truly brings you joy. Think about those moments in your life where you felt completely alive. What were you doing? Who were you with? Sometimes, our passion is buried in past experiences, just waiting to be rediscovered.

And here's something important: Passion doesn't have to be big or world-changing. Some people are passionate about astrophysics, while others love knitting tiny sweaters for their cats (seriously, there are Instagram accounts dedicated to this). Whatever it is, if it makes you happy and drives you, it's valid.

Now, a little secret about passion that no one really talks about is that just because you're passionate about something doesn't mean you'll love every single moment of it. Shocking, right? Even when you've found your passion, there will be days when it's hard work, when you're frustrated, or just not feeling it. It's kind of like those days when you really don't want to go to the gym, even though you're passionate about fitness.

Passion doesn't erase the challenges—it gives you the drive to push through them. Just look at Steve Jobs. He was wildly passionate about technology and innovation, but that doesn't mean he enjoyed every late-night coding session or every setback. Passion doesn't guarantee 24/7 fun; it guarantees commitment. It's that thing that makes you show up, even when it's tough because deep down, it's worth it.

Once you've found something you're passionate about, the next challenge is keeping that flame alive. Passion needs to be nurtured, just like any important relationship in your life. One great way to keep the fire going is by setting goals—both big and small. If you love writing, commit to finishing a certain number of pages every week. If fitness is your passion, sign up for a race or a challenge that keeps you motivated.

Mixing things up can help, too. If your passion is starting to feel stale, challenge yourself to try new things within that space. If you love cooking, try tackling a cuisine you've never cooked before. Passion thrives on growth and challenge, so don't be afraid to step out of your comfort zone now and then.

Another important aspect of keeping your passion alive is surrounding yourself with passionate people. Passion is contagious. When you're around others who are fired up about their own passions, it has a way of reigniting your own flame.

But let's not forget that rest is important too. Burnout is real, even when it comes to things you love. It's okay to take a break, step back, and recharge when you need to. Passion is a long game, not a sprint. The last thing you want is to burn out before you've fully embraced what makes you come alive.

Once you're in the groove of living your passion, the real magic happens when that passion turns into purpose. Passion is awesome, but when you take that passion and use it to positively impact others or the world around you, that's where the real joy and fulfillment kick in.

How can you take your passion and make it something bigger than yourself? Maybe you love teaching and can use that passion to mentor someone who's just starting out. If you're passionate about music, maybe you can share your talent in a community setting. If you care deeply about the environment, your passion could turn into a movement to help educate others.

The beautiful thing about passion is that it's not just for you—it's a gift that can inspire and lift others up, too. And that's where the real impact of passion is felt.

Here's something that might take the pressure off: Passion doesn't have to be your career. There's this myth floating around that if you're passionate about something, you have to turn it into a full-time job. Not true! It's perfectly okay to have a regular 9-to-5 job and pursue your passions on the side. In fact, sometimes keeping your passion separate from your work can make it even more enjoyable because there's no pressure to make money from it.

Passion doesn't have to be your paycheck. It can be your weekend activity, your side project, or something you make time for in small doses. As long as you're making room for it, you're doing it right.

And remember, passion—just like life—isn't a straight line. It's more like a roller coaster with highs, lows, twists, and unexpected turns. One day, you might feel unstoppable, and the next, you might wonder why you ever cared so much. That's completely normal. Passion evolves as you do. What lit you up five years ago might not be what fires you up now, and that's okay.

At the end of the day, passion is about finding something that makes you come alive. It's about waking up with purpose, knowing that there's something you love and care about enough to pour your time and energy into. And once you've found it, hold onto it, nurture it, and let it guide you in creating a life that's full of joy, fulfillment, and excitement.

In the following headings, I will use my children's life journey to better illustrate "passion" and how it can be ignited. We will see how challenges can end up being passion and how little interest can grow into passion.

OUTSIDE THE LINES

Let's start with my middle child, Toni. She's an incredible young lady who struggled as a kid with a few things. My wife and I knew about the obvious things, like her difficulties with reading and speaking. We used to joke that she had the "Teletubbies spirit" because she would mimic the characters from that kid's show. It was funny, but it also made us a little concerned.

I remember praying that she would grow out of it, and man, did she really grow out of it big time? Toni and I co-authored two books together, *COPO, the Teen Book* and *COPO, the Kids Book*. I set a goal for myself to write at least a book with my kids, and Toni was the first to join me on that journey. The transformation I've witnessed in her life is nothing short of miraculous. When she was younger, getting her to say even a few words was a challenge, but now? She CAN'T STOP! It's mind-blowing to think about how she went from being so quiet to being able to express herself clearly and confidently.

What's even more impressive is that she didn't have much exposure to reading at first. Her comprehension was always high, but phonics just didn't click for her for a long time. We enrolled her in an after-school program to help her improve her reading skills. It was tight for her, and I could relate to it because I struggled with reading as a child, too.

Her mother, on the other hand, was an amazing reader. I'm talking straight A's all through school. If she got a B, you'd think the world was ending! If I got a C, the whole block should be on fire, with Piñatas filled with starburst and skittles and letter confetti all over the place.

In an interview we did after our books were released, Toni revealed some challenges I had no idea she was facing. She had foot surgery as a preteen, which left her in a wheelchair for a whole school year. During that time, she endured bullying. She went on to say that while her siblings were out playing sports and living life, she felt isolated, depressed, and alone.

But then, something pretty dope happened. One day, she picked up a book, and it was like a light bulb went on. Suddenly, the words made sense, and she dove headfirst into reading. It was as if someone flipped a switch, and she couldn't stop! Toni started devouring books daily! Just like her older sister, Adrienne, who shared that same passion for reading. We used to punish them by taking away their books. In a nerdy, strange way, that became the worst punishment possible for her. Before we knew it, Toni was reading thick novels and engaging in deep, meaningful conversations with adults by the time she was 14.

One day, I asked her what she wanted to be when she grew up. Without skipping a beat, she said, "I want to be a teacher."

As she got a little older, I pressed her for more details. "What age group do you want to teach?" I asked. Her response was so insightful: "I want to teach kids before they get to third grade." Intrigued, I asked why before third grade. She went on to say something I never forgot. When they leave the third grade, they have to start getting too serious. Sit up straight, stop making random noises with body parts, laugh at everything, and ultimately start drawing within the lines. I want to catch them while they can be most creative." I could see that passion for nurturing creativity shining through her words. Fast forward ten years later, and Toni not only went to school to become a teacher, but she also became a reading specialist.

I've always said that God has a funny way of showing us how much we don't know. Here was my daughter, who once struggled to find her voice, now teaching others how to read and appreciate the beauty of words. She worked various jobs along the way, from Panera to kid ministry, but eventually found her sweet spot where her passion, occupation, and calling all aligned as an elementary school teacher. I couldn't be prouder of what God has done in her life. This sixteen-year-old absolutely blew my mind with this, and I've been using it in sermons, counseling, and coaching ever since.

You see, passion isn't something that can always be confined within neat little boundaries. It doesn't always follow a straight path or unfold according to a perfect plan. Toni is a living proof of this.

One of the most remarkable things about passion is that it often reveals itself when you least expect it. For Toni, that moment came when she picked up a book one day, and suddenly, everything clicked. It was like watching a flower bloom overnight. She went from being the quiet kid who struggled with words to devouring books and engaging in deep conversations, often with people twice her age. The same girl who once couldn't find her voice became a lover of words and stories. If someone had told me when she was younger that one day we'd write books together, I would have laughed—and yet, here we are.

Passion isn't always obvious at first, and it doesn't always come easily. But when it does show up, it can transform a person's entire world. Toni's love for reading grew into something much bigger than just a personal hobby. It became her calling. By the time she was in her teens, she knew without a doubt that she wanted to become a teacher. And not just any teacher—she wanted to reach children before they hit third grade, the point at which, according to her, kids start getting "too serious" and are forced to draw inside the lines, both figuratively and literally.

This insight blew me away. As a teenager, she already had a deep understanding of how creativity works and how crucial those early years of learning and playfulness are. Toni wanted to nurture that pure, unfiltered creativity in young kids, encouraging them to stay imaginative before the system teaches them otherwise. That's when I knew her passion wasn't just about reading. It was about helping others discover their own potential, especially during those critical years when kids are still free to dream without limits.

Fast forward a few years, and Toni followed through on her passion with laser-focused determination. She became a reading specialist, guiding young students through the same struggles she once faced. It's amazing how the very thing that caused her so much frustration as a child became the foundation of her career. This is something I often reflect on when I talk about passion—it's not always a smooth journey, but sometimes your greatest challenges turn into your greatest passions.

What I love most about her life is that it reminds me how passion doesn't have to fit into the standard mold. It doesn't have to be neat and tidy or even logical at first. It's something that grows and evolves with time, sometimes taking unexpected routes. Toni's passion for teaching and reading may have started with a personal struggle, but it developed into a powerful purpose: to make a difference in the lives of others, especially the kids who might be struggling in the same ways she once did.

Toni's passion for reading and teaching is also a reminder that passion doesn't always announce itself loudly. It can start as a whisper, a small interest or curiosity, and then, one day, it's a roar that you can't ignore. I think a lot of people get stuck waiting for that one big moment when passion will knock them over like a wave. But more often than not, passion grows slowly, like a seed planted in rocky soil that somehow takes root and blossoms.

For Toni, it wasn't just about discovering what she loved. It was about finding meaning in her passion and using her experiences to shape her future. Her passion for reading didn't just transform her life—it gave her the tools to help others find their own voices, just as she found hers. And that's the incredible power of passion. It has this ripple effect, touching not just your life but the lives of others in ways you might never expect.

Looking back, I'm beyond proud of the lady Toni has become. The girl who once struggled to say a few words is now helping other children find their voices, teaching them to read, and showing them that there's so much more to learning than just following the rules and staying inside the lines.

Remember, passion doesn't always start with fireworks. Sometimes, it starts quietly, in moments of struggle and frustration, and slowly grows into something that can light up the world.

MUSIC TO MY EARS

Now, let's talk about my youngest daughter, Erin. She's a creative old soul in her own right, but she faced her own struggles with learning. I'd describe her as "street smart," and she had this unique way of dealing with school. One night, while we were at home getting quiet for the night, we heard some noise coming from upstairs. It sounded like an acapella neo-soul session was going down in the attic, but we knew Jill Scott was not upstairs. It was only one person that it could be. I yelled upstairs, "Erin!!!!!!!! Come down here!!!"

We asked, almost as if we were concerned, "Was that you upstairs?" She said yes. You can sing???!!! My wife Dawn and I both kept asking. We're like, who is this alien in our home? After a lot of begging and pleading, she finally sang for us, and let me tell you, when she opened her mouth, I knew she had found her passion.

Erin started singing on our worship team at our church. We understood that the life of a musician could be tough, and we all knew that this girl had a special gift. All the way through high school, she rocked talent shows, school events, worship, and youth conferences. She picked up the guitar, and after a smooth 2 classes, she started teaching herself how to play. She was really determined to pursue music, and she was really good at it.

While music came naturally to her, the school remained a challenge for her, so we made the decision to move her to an aviation school. You might think that's a strange choice, but it turned out to be the perfect fit! With a different culture and environment, Erin started to thrive academically and socially as she is a very soft-spoken, extreme extrovert in most settings.

From an early age, I also knew that Erin had a knack for cooking. We'd spend time in the kitchen together, playing with recipes and

Erin and her sister competing in cooking challenges. One year, we entered a citywide cooking competition; she was in the teen category, and I was in the adult division. We both won! That was a pivotal moment for me; it was when I realized that Erin had serious culinary talent and could potentially turn it into a career.

By 10th grade, Erin signed up for cooking classes, and by the time she graduated, she had credits towards her associate's degree and certifications in culinary arts while in high school. We saw her passion and her skill set for cooking become equally as good as her singing. She went on to college, finished her degree in one of the top culinary schools in the country, and became a private chef for extremely wealthy people. In the least expected place, she discovered a passion for cooking. It was a cool journey to witness her find what she loved to do.

Like I said earlier, passion doesn't always look the way we expect it to. Erin didn't follow a predictable path—who knew that a kid who thrived on creative cooking challenges and singing neo-soul in the attic would one day become a private chef? But that's the beauty of passion. It has its own timing, its own rhythm, and when you follow it, it can take you places you never dreamed of going.

When I think about Erin and her path, what stands out most to me is how her passions for both music and cooking didn't come from external pressure or expectations. It wasn't about getting good grades, impressing teachers, or following the footsteps of someone else. Erin's passion was entirely her own. And that's something I think is really important for all of us to understand: passion can't be forced. It doesn't always show up in the areas we think it should—like school, for example—but that doesn't make it any less valid or important.

Too often, we expect passion to align perfectly with what's considered "successful" by society's standards. But Erin is a great example of how passion can grow and flourish in unexpected ways.

Who would have guessed that Erin, the girl who struggled academically, would thrive in an aviation school and later excel in the culinary arts? It's proof to us all that passion doesn't have to fit into a pre-made box. It can flow out in all directions, sometimes leading to music, sometimes to cooking, or maybe even both at once.

What I loved most about watching Erin discover her passions was how they each began as small sparks—just fun things she enjoyed doing. Singing was something she did when no one was around, and cooking was something she enjoyed when she felt creative. But those small sparks became flames because she didn't ignore them. Erin nurtured her passions, whether it was spending hours in the kitchen or teaching herself guitar in her bedroom. She didn't wait for someone to tell her, "This is what you should do," she just followed her heart. And that's one of the most powerful lessons we can learn about passion: it grows when you give it space to breathe and develop.

As Erin honed her talents, it became clear that passion doesn't just stay as an internal feeling. It evolves, it matures, and it starts to show itself in your actions. Her passions for music and cooking didn't remain hobbies; they transformed into skills, ones that she worked at and invested time in. Passion is about more than just loving something—it's about putting in the effort, the dedication, and the time to get better at it. Erin worked hard to develop her voice, her guitar skills, and her cooking techniques, and she became exceptional at both.

And while Erin's story is her own, it speaks to a universal truth: passion often finds its way into our lives in unexpected places. Erin didn't grow up saying, "I'm going to be a chef." It was something that evolved naturally over time. The joy she found in cooking with me, the competitions, the classes—it all came together to create this path that she hadn't planned but one she wholeheartedly embraced.

I remember how she lit up when she won that citywide cooking competition. It was as if something clicked for her like she realized she was really good at this—and more importantly, that she loved it. That's what passion does: it not only gives you a purpose, but it also fuels you to keep going, to keep pushing forward, even when the road isn't easy.

There's also something to be said about the relationship between passion and purpose. Passion often leads us to our purpose in life, even if we don't recognize it at first. Erin's love for cooking led her to become a private chef, which not only gave her a fulfilling career but also allowed her to use her creativity and talents to bring joy to others. Whether she was preparing a dish for a family or putting together a meal for a large event, she was using her gifts to serve others. And isn't that what passion is all about? It's about finding what you love and using it to make a difference in whatever way that looks for you.

I think back to the early days of Erin's musical journey and how she would quietly practice upstairs, away from everyone, until she found the confidence to share her talent. Her passion for singing was never about fame or recognition. It was always about the pure joy of expressing herself through music. And when she started to share that gift with others—whether at church or in talent shows—you could see how much it meant to her and to those around her. Passion, at its core, is contagious. When you pursue what you love, it inspires others to do the same.

Erin's life is a powerful reminder that passion isn't about following the most obvious or straightforward path. It's about listening to that voice inside you, the one that tells you to keep going even when things don't make sense. It's about exploring different avenues, being open to change, and embracing the unexpected. Whether it's singing or cooking, passion isn't limited to one thing. It can show up in multiple areas of our lives, and that's the beauty of it.

Passion doesn't have to follow the rules. It doesn't have to be about getting the highest grades or climbing the corporate ladder.

Passion is about finding what lights you up inside and pursuing it, even if it takes you in a completely different direction than you thought you'd go. Erin's journey from singing in the attic to cooking for some of the wealthiest people around is proof of that. She didn't follow a typical path, but she followed her passion—and that's what made all the difference.

As her father, watching her pursue these passions has been an incredible journey for me, too. It's a reminder that each of us has our own path and that passion is often the thing that helps us find it. It doesn't always make sense at first, but when you follow your heart, you end up exactly where you're supposed to be. For Erin, it was a kitchen and a stage, and I couldn't be prouder of the woman she had become.

THE SHIFT

Now, let's shift gears and talk about my oldest son, Anthony. I had him when I was just 16, and to be honest, we grew up together in a lot of ways. I was active in his life, yes, but often away for long stretches. As he grew older, we had some tough conversations about my absences. I remember showing up at his house one day, feeling overwhelmed with guilt about not being there for him when he needed me. But his response was a healing balm for my soul: "Dad, I get it. I get it. If you hadn't left, you wouldn't be here for me now."

"Sometimes pursuing your passion means blindly leaping into uncertainty."

Anthony is incredibly gifted when it comes to technology, music, and boxing. Early on, I realized he had a natural talent for tech. So I would take him to work with me and toss a computer in front of him, show him how to take it apart, and put it back together. He was only 12, and it was like finding water. But here's the thing—he grew up in the hood, surrounded by influences that could easily lead him astray. For a while, the streets were calling him, and he answered. His music often reflected that struggle. Following my footsteps in many ways. He, too, became a teen father of my first grandson. Later, he and Monique had my granddaughter.

Even through all the craziness the life of a trap rapper would bring, I could see Anthony searching for something more meaningful. He started talking about God and seeking a relationship with Him. I didn't lead him to Christ; he found Him on his own, and it was a dope journey to witness.

As he began to find out who he was, he also saw his passion for the street start to refocus. I think he realized he had a knack for boxing and creating music videos, but those weren't the root of his passion. Something shifted in his 30's. He felt a calling to make an impact in his community. He became involved with the local urban league, working as a specialist in anti-violence. Seeing the spark in his eyes when he talks about his work is incredible. You can feel the passion radiating from him! He found it... He found his passion.

Passion is an extraordinary force that drives us forward when the road is unclear and fuels us when life feels overwhelming. For Anthony, that passion had always been bubbling beneath the surface, sometimes hidden by the challenges of his environment, his circumstances, and the tumultuous path he walked in his youth. But once it was discovered, it was unstoppable.

But passion, while powerful, is not always linear. It doesn't follow a set path or a clear trajectory. Anthony was also a product of his environment, and like many young men growing up in the hood, he wrestled with the allure of the streets. His passion for technology was real, but so was the pull of the world around him. His music became an outlet, reflecting his inner turmoil and the duality of the person he was becoming—a person with immense potential, navigating a landscape of challenges that could have easily consumed him.

Yet, even in the darkest moments, passion has a way of steering us toward the light. Anthony's journey into the world of music, and later boxing, was another chapter in his search for purpose. Boxing, in particular, became more than just a sport—it became a way for him to channel his energy, his frustration, and even his pain. And though boxing and music brought him a level of satisfaction, they weren't his final destination.

As he entered his 30s, there was a shift. It's common for people to go through periods of self-reflection as they age, and Anthony was no exception. He started to look inward, asking himself deeper questions about his place in the world, his legacy, and his impact on those around him. What once felt like passion began to morph into something more profound—a calling. He realized that while boxing and music were important parts of his journey, they weren't the endgame.

Passion is like a compass, always pointing us in the right direction, even when the destination isn't immediately clear. For Anthony, the compass began to point toward his community. He started to understand that his true passion wasn't in the ring or in a recording studio—it was in making a difference. His involvement with the local urban league and his work in anti-violence initiatives didn't just give him fulfillment; it ignited a fire in him that burned brighter than anything he had ever experienced before.

It's one thing to have a passion for something, but it's another thing entirely to have a passion that is tied to service and community. Anthony's journey brought him full circle, from a young boy with a talent for technology to a man who found meaning in giving back. His passion evolved from self-expression to service, from individual achievement to collective progress. In many ways, it mirrored my own journey—the struggle to find purpose, the winding roads, the mistakes, and ultimately, the passion for urban ministry.

Watching Anthony discover his passion was, for me, one of the most fulfilling experiences as a father. I wasn't there for him in all the ways I should have been when he was younger, but seeing him grow into the man he is today—someone who understands that passion is more than just what you're good at, but what you're willing to sacrifice for—makes me feel like we've both come a long way.

When Anthony speaks about his work now, there's an unmistakable light in his eyes. That same light that I saw when he was a boy, sitting in front of a computer, is now shining even brighter. But this time, it's not just about him—it's about the people he's helping, the lives he's touching, and the community he's building. His passion has grown, evolved, and become something truly powerful.

"Our Passion is not about what we do but who we become"

It's been said that "your passion is waiting for your courage to catch up," and for Anthony, that courage came when he decided to step away from the distractions of his youth and step into something bigger than himself. He found his passion not by looking for it but by living, learning, and allowing life to shape him. And now, that passion is shaping the world around him in ways that I know will have a lasting impact for generations to come.

In the end, passion isn't just about what we do; it's about who we become. Anthony is a perfect example of that truth. He is living proof that no matter where we start, our passion has the power to guide us to where we are truly meant to be. And for that, I couldn't be more proud.

I FEEL LIKE BUSTIN LOOSE

You know that feeling when you're scrolling through your social media feed, and something just hits you out of nowhere, sparking a need to do something? I'm not talking about something that comes and goes. That feeling that you just can't shake. That could very well be that God Given passion bubbling up!

Often, our God's passions are tied to our deepest emotions, hurts, and personal experiences. They are often just waiting for the right time to start to bust through the ground. Like the seed of a flower that is planted into the dirt, passion has been strategically placed inside of you by the God of the universe. When the time is right, that first sprout will burst out of the ground screaming, "Freedom!!!"

Anthony had a deep love for the street, but he did not fully understand it until he had enough. And Erin literally opened her mouth and let the good times flow. In its time, when it is ready, you have to stop fighting against what the Lord deposited in you and let it out and let your passion shine.

Think about Moses for a second. He had a pretty complicated life. He was a Hebrew boy raised as an Egyptian, and he still felt a deep connection to his people. One day, he saw an Egyptian beating a Hebrew slave, and it was like a switch flipped in him. He was so overwhelmed with emotion that he acted on impulse and ended up killing the Egyptian. This is a classic example of what happens when our passions are underdeveloped, and we let 'em run loose prematurely without any guidance from the Lord. In most cases, when we release premature passion on the earth, it often leads to choices we regret.

Proverbs 19:2 says, "Desire without knowledge is not good; Haste Makes mistakes." It's a solid reminder that while our passions can motivate us, we really need to mix in some biblical wisdom. When we let our feelings take control without checking in with God, we might miss the mark and stray away from what we're truly meant to do.

Like Moses, that raw passion inside us comes directly from God. Our passions are part of His creative design. They are meant to be expressed in ways that reflect His love and kindness. When we graciously hand our passions at his feet, He will turn our hurts into healing, our anger into action, and our frustrations into something that impacts our family, community, and world. I can't say this enough...

As we navigate our passions, it's so important to invite the Lord's wisdom into the mix, as He's more than willing to nurture that passion and release us into action when the time is right for us to get it crackin'. When we do that, ensure that our actions line up with His heart, leading us to create lasting change in our lives and the lives of others.

So, feel free to embrace your passions as gifts from God. Instead of just reacting to what we feel, we can turn those emotions into intentional actions that transform the world around us.

Passion is one of the most powerful forces we possess, but it's not something we should approach carelessly. Just like Moses, who allowed his unbridled passion to push him into a decision he later regretted, our passion, when mishandled or released prematurely, can lead us down paths we didn't intend to travel. It's crucial to remember that while our passion is God-given, it also requires cultivation and wisdom.

Think of passion like a fire. When it's well-tended, it provides warmth, light, and comfort. But when left uncontrolled, it can quickly become destructive, consuming everything around it. Many of us feel a burning desire to do something impactful—to change our lives, the lives of others, or even the world. But without proper guidance and timing, that same burning desire can lead us into trouble.

One of the most important lessons I've learned about passion is the importance of timing. Passion often feels urgent, like something that needs to be acted on immediately, but God works on a different timeline than we do. Our passions are often tied to our deepest wounds and experiences, and sometimes, we're tempted to act on them as soon as we feel that emotional surge. However, God doesn't just give us passion; He also gives us wisdom and patience so that when the time is right, we can unleash that passion in a way that makes the most significant impact.

This process of waiting is challenging. It's not easy to sit on something that feels so intense, especially when you feel that God has placed it inside you for a reason. But waiting doesn't mean inactivity; it means preparation. The Lord doesn't just give us passion without the tools to fulfill it. While we wait, He is often preparing us for the moment when our passion will intersect with His purpose.

Take Anthony, for example. His passion for technology, boxing, and music was apparent from a young age. But that passion alone wasn't enough to guide him in the right direction. It wasn't until he went through some tough life experiences and matured emotionally and spiritually that his passion became more focused. It evolved from being about self-expression or survival into something deeper— helping his community and making a positive impact through his work in anti-violence. His passion became not just a source of personal fulfillment but a source of healing for others.

This shift is key. Passion, when aligned with God's purpose, becomes a tool for transformation. And this transformation isn't just internal; it extends outward, creating a ripple effect in the lives of those around us. We can see this clearly in Anthony's story. He started with a passion for the streets, but over time, the Lord redirected that passion toward something more profound and meaningful. His journey reminds us that passion isn't just about what makes us feel good or excited; it's about what we are called to do to better the world around us.

The challenge, of course, is learning how to recognize when our passion is ready to be acted upon. Having a passion is not enough. We need knowledge, guidance, and discernment to ensure that our passion leads us to the right place. When we rush into things without first seeking God's counsel, we often end up making mistakes or veering off course.

Moses' story is a perfect illustration of this. His passion for justice was real, but when he acted on it impulsively, without waiting for God's timing, it led to him fleeing into the desert for 40 years. During that time, however, the Lord didn't let Moses' passion die.

Instead, He refined it. By the time Moses returned to Egypt to lead his people to freedom, his passion was no longer raw and uncontrolled. It had been tempered by wisdom, humility, and a deep relationship with the Lord. His passion became not just a personal mission but a divine calling that changed the course of history.

In our own lives, we must be willing to undergo that same refinement. We need to trust that God is working in us even when it feels like we're stuck or when we feel the urge to act immediately. Passion isn't a sprint; it's a marathon. The preparation is just as important as the execution.

So, what does this mean for us today? It means that we need to stop fighting against the passions the Lord has placed in us. Often, we try to suppress or ignore them, especially if they don't seem to fit neatly into the life we've planned. But passion isn't meant to be ignored. It's meant to be nurtured and brought to life at the right time. When we let go of control and hand our passions over to God, trusting Him to guide us, we will see them grow and blossom in ways we never imagined.

God's timing is perfect, and His wisdom is incomparable. When we align our passions with His purpose, we open ourselves up to becoming instruments of change, not just for ourselves but for our families, our communities, and the world.

So embrace your passion. Let it be a reminder that the Lord has placed something uniquely beautiful inside of you. And when the time is right—when your passion has been refined, matured, and guided by His wisdom—step boldly into your calling. There's a world waiting to be changed, and your passion is part of that change.

Life Application: We must be willing to reflect on the issues, injustices, or challenges that stir the deepest emotions within us. These passions, when surrendered to God, can become the fuel that drives us to fulfill our unique callings. By embracing our hurts and allowing God to redeem them, we open the door for Him to use our stories in powerful ways.

REFLECTION QUESTIONS

- What are the deepest passions and desires of your heart? How have they been shaped by your experiences, both positive and negative?

- In what ways have you seen your passions lead you astray or cause you to stray from God's will? How can you learn to surrender those desires to the Lord?

- When have you witnessed your passions being redeemed and redirected by God for His purposes? What did that process look like, and how did it impact your life and the lives of others?

- Who are the people in your life who can provide wisdom and accountability as you seek to align your passions with God's will? How can you cultivate those relationships?

- What practical steps can you take to regularly examine your passions, allowing God to refine and redirect them? How can you make space in your life for Him to speak to the desires of your heart?

CALL TO ACTION

Take some time to prayerfully reflect on the passions and desires of your heart. Ask the God of the universe to reveal any areas where those longings may be leading you astray or hindering your ability to fulfill the calling he has on your life. Seek out mentors in your community who can provide accountability and encouragement as you learn to align your passions with God's purpose.

- Reflect on Your Life Experiences that shape your worldview
- Create a timeline of significant events in your life, both positive and negative.
- Write down how each event made you feel and if it sparked a desire to change something in your community or your own life.
- Make a list of social issues that resonate with you.
- Next to each issue, write down why it matters to you and any experiences you've had related to it.
- List your top five skills and talents.
- Consider how these can be applied to the social issues you identified earlier.

Chapter Four
OPPORTUNITY

Let's talk about something we all love—opportunity. That magical, amazing concept can change your life or at the very least give you an excuse to get out of bed in the morning. You know, the thing your motivational Instagram quotes are always raving about. "When one door closes, another opens," they say. It's all very poetic until you realize the door that opened leads to a dentist's office or a Monday morning meeting that could have been an email.

But hey, that's still an opportunity, right? And that's the thing about opportunities—they come in all shapes and sizes, and sometimes, they're disguised as things you'd rather avoid. But when you recognize them, seize them, and run with them? Oh boy, that's when the magic happens. So buckle up because, in this chapter, we will look at opportunities—how to find them, embrace them, and maybe even laugh at them when they show up in the most unexpected ways.

Have you ever heard the phrase "opportunity knocks?" Well, here's the catch—they don't tell you how hard it knocks. Sometimes, it's more of a polite tap, barely louder than a whisper, while you're binge-watching Netflix. The problem is, most of us are waiting for an opportunity to knock like a neighbor who's locked out of their house —loud, frantic, and impossible to ignore.

But no, opportunity mostly doesn't come like that. It doesn't always show up with a neon sign or a parade of fireworks. Often, it's in the little things—a casual conversation, an unexpected job offer, or that random email you almost deleted because you thought it was spam.

The key is learning to listen. Pay attention to those quiet knocks because they might be the ones that lead to the biggest changes. And trust me. You do not want to be the person who missed out on the next big thing because you were too busy ignoring the tap-tap-tap of opportunity while scrolling through TikTok.

Ah, Yes, we all love opportunities until we realize they usually require effort. It's like ordering dessert at a fancy restaurant and finding out you have to assemble it yourself. Sure, you get to eat it in the end, but only after a few frustrating minutes of trying to figure out how to balance a strawberry on a piece of artisanal chocolate.

The same goes for opportunities. They often come dressed as hard work, and that's where people get tripped up. You might see a chance for a promotion at work but hesitate because it means longer hours. Or maybe you want to start a side hustle, but the thought of giving up your Saturday mornings makes you cringe.

Here's the thing that most people don't understand, opportunities and hard work are best friends. They hang out together all the time. You can't really have one without the other. But don't worry—once you dive in, you'll usually find that the work isn't as bad as you thought. Plus, there's the payoff at the end, and who doesn't love that?

Raise your hand if you've ever said, "I'm just waiting for the right time." (I know I have.) But the truth is that there is no "right time." It's a myth, like Bigfoot or those unicorn frappuccinos that actually taste good.

We all have this fantasy that the stars will align, the universe will send us a sign, and suddenly we'll feel 100% ready to take on a new challenge. But in reality, life doesn't work that way. The perfect time to seize an opportunity is now, even if you feel unprepared or scared or like you really need a nap first.

It's easy to talk yourself out of things, to say you'll do it when you have more money, more experience, more whatever. But opportunities don't wait around for you to feel ready. They show up when they feel like it, and it's up to you to jump on board or risk missing out. (And who wants FOMO, right?)

Here's another interesting fact, opportunities and failure are also buddies. If opportunities hang out with hard work, then failure is the wise old sage that tags along to make sure you learn something. And you will fail sometimes. It's inevitable. But the good news? Failing doesn't mean you missed your chance; it means you're getting closer to success.

Think about it this way, every failure is like a dress rehearsal for the real thing. You're just ironing out the kinks before you take the stage for your big moment. So, instead of fearing failure, embrace it. Each mistake is a stepping stone, and before you know it, you'll be running full speed toward success—laughing at all those little faceplants along the way. (Just maybe wear knee pads. Metaphorical ones, of course. Or real ones if you're clumsy like me.)

Sometimes, the best opportunities come disguised as total disasters. Maybe you lose your job, or a big project falls apart, or you spill coffee all over your brand-new shirt five minutes before an important meeting. It's tempting to think, "Why me?!"

But if you look closer, you'll often find a hidden silver lining. Losing your job might push you to pursue a passion you'd been neglecting. A failed project could lead to a new approach that works even better. And that coffee spill? Well, at least you have a funny story to tell at the office party.

While leading the IT department for the American Red Cross Grand Rapids Chapter, I met a dude named Jordan O'Neil. He is one of the most innovative leaders I've met to date. 20 years later, I am happy to call him a friend. He went on to start an organization called Failure Lab and has an amazing perspective on failure.

"Failure taught me lessons that success never could. It's easy to celebrate wins, but real growth comes from navigating the messy, uncomfortable aftermath of a fall. That's why I started a storytelling event series called Failure Lab—to create a space where people could share their failures openly, without judgment, and explore the raw, real, and relatable moments that make us human. Each Failure Lab story ends at a crucial, unresolved point, encouraging the audience to reflect, empathize, and become part of the experience. It's not about prescribing lessons but rather about fostering self-inquiry and connections through shared struggles. I've seen how these moments of vulnerability transform into powerful tools for personal and

collective growth. Failure Lab reminds us that stumbling is part of the
journey—the true test is how we rise. By embracing failure, we discover
the strength to inspire change and build resilience within ourselves and
our communities."

~ Jordan O'Neil ~

I was humbled when I was asked to speak at one of these events. By God's grace, I've spoken at national conferences with 5000 people, appeared on international TV & radio shows, and even did a TEDx Talk. I've never experienced anything like this. To simply own your failure in the community. No solutions, no excuses. Just admit the failure, walk off the stage, and deal with it. The emotion you feel is unexplainable. You want to take it all back, yet you feel relieved that you just said it... Yeah, I failed, and so what!?!? I have seen other speakers and audience members weep during the few moments of silence between each speaker. It's normal to fail and take time to reflect on what happened. It's also normal to dust yourself off and get up and get back at it.

The point is that not all opportunities come wrapped in a shiny bow. Sometimes, they look like chaos. But with the right mindset, you can turn a setback into a setup for something amazing. Just remember, life has a funny way of steering you in the right direction

—especially when you're busy cursing that coffee stain.

You've probably heard the phrase "Carpe Diem," which means "Seize the day." Sounds fancy, right? Sounds like something you'd say while sipping on an over-priced latte with my pinky out. But in reality, seizing the day just means grabbing hold of opportunities before they slip away.

We all know that regret is a terrible feeling. It's like when you pass on dessert at a restaurant, and then you spend the next hour watching your friend eat their grandma's cream cheese pound cake while you cry inside. Don't let that be you when it comes to opportunities.

When something feels right—or even if it just feels interesting—go for it. Take the chance. Say yes to that new job, that travel opportunity, that wacky business idea that makes your heart race a little. Sure, it might be scary, and yes, you might fail. But you'll never know unless you try.

And hey, even if it doesn't work out, at least you won't be stuck wondering "what if" for the rest of your life. (And you can always console yourself with molten lava cake. No regrets there.)

Opportunities are like Pokémon—you've gotta catch 'em all. Or at least catch the ones that matter. They're everywhere, even when you're not looking for them. The key is to stay open, be curious, and say yes more often than you say no.

Remember, not every opportunity will come with a flashing neon sign, and sometimes they'll show up looking like hard work, failure, or a big ol' mess. But if you keep your eyes peeled and your mind open, you'll find that opportunities are all around you—just waiting for you to take the leap.

And who knows? That leap could be the start of something incredible. Or, at the very least, it could make your Monday a little more interesting. So go ahead, open that door. Opportunity's knocking—don't leave it waiting.

STEPPING OUT IN FAITH

"Opportunity: Stepping Out in Faith is about taking that leap when the time comes."

We've all heard the saying, "You miss 100% of the shots you don't take." That might be a sports analogy, but it rings true in every aspect of life. Opportunity is that shot, that moment when you stand at a crossroads, faced with a decision that could take you somewhere amazing or terrifying. And when it comes to opportunity, one thing is for sure: it often requires a leap of faith.

But let's be honest—stepping out in faith is easier said than done. It's hard to take the plunge when you're staring into the unknown. Sure, everyone loves a good "rags to riches" story where the hero takes a wild risk, and everything works out beautifully. But when it's you, and the stakes are real? That's when the nerves set in, and suddenly, the comfort zone feels a whole lot more appealing. The couch seems comfier, the current job safer, and the dream you've been holding onto feels just a little too ambitious. So, how do you step out in faith and seize opportunity when all the odds seem stacked against you?

Let's start with this: no one is 100% ready for the big opportunities that come their way. In fact, waiting until you're "ready" is a surefire way to watch your opportunities pass you by. Stepping out in faith means accepting that there will always be uncertainty, and that's okay. You're never going to have everything perfectly lined up—your ducks will rarely be in a row. If you're waiting for a sign that it's the right time, here it is: the perfect time is now.

One of the greatest myths about opportunity is that we'll feel confident and capable before we make the leap. This couldn't be further from the truth. The reality is that growth and confidence happen after you step out, not before. When you take a leap of faith, it's like building a plane as you're flying it. Scary, right? But that's the beauty of it. You learn, grow, and adapt as you go. That discomfort you feel? It's a sign you're moving in the right direction. Growth doesn't happen when you're comfortable.

"Feel fear and do it anyway"

Remember, faith isn't the absence of fear; it's action despite fear. Stepping out in faith doesn't mean you're not scared—it just means you're willing to move forward even though you're scared. Fear is natural. It's what makes us human. But if you let fear dictate your choices, you'll find yourself standing still while opportunities pass you by. There's a quote that goes, "Feel the fear and do it anyway." That's the essence of stepping out in faith. You acknowledge the fear, but you don't let it stop you.

And don't forget I said earlier that opportunity and failure often go hand-in-hand. People who seize opportunities know that failure is part of the deal. They expect it, learn from it, and keep moving. It's not failure that defines them; it's their resilience. When you step out in faith, you have to accept that things won't always go as planned. In fact, they rarely do. However, each misstep is an opportunity to learn something new and adjust the course. It's like hiking up a mountain: sometimes, you have to backtrack a bit or take a different path, but as long as you keep climbing, you'll get to the top.

This brings us to another important aspect of opportunity: trust. Stepping out in faith requires trust, not just in yourself but also in the process. There's a certain level of surrender that comes with taking big risks. You do your best to prepare, plan, and execute, but at some point, you have to let go of the need for control. Things won't always happen the way you imagined, and that's okay. Sometimes, you have to trust that what's meant for you will come, even if the journey looks different than you expected.

It's also crucial to surround yourself with people who encourage you to take those leaps of faith. We've all had moments where we doubted ourselves, but having a support system can make all the difference. Whether it's a friend or family member, find someone who will remind you that you're capable and push you when you need that extra nudge. There's strength in community, and when you have people cheering you on, it's easier to step into the unknown.

And speaking of the unknown—don't let it paralyze you. Yes, stepping out in faith means embracing uncertainty, but it also means welcoming possibility. Too often, we let the fear of the unknown stop us from pursuing opportunities. We focus on what could go wrong instead of what could go right. But what if, instead of worrying about all the potential pitfalls, you thought about all the incredible outcomes that could happen if you took the leap?

Think about all the things you've accomplished in your life so far. Chances are, many of them came from moments when you took a risk or stepped outside your comfort zone. Maybe it was going for a job you didn't think you were qualified for, moving to a new city, or starting a relationship. In hindsight, those leaps of faith likely led to some of your greatest personal growth and success. The same will be true for the opportunities that await you now—you just have to be willing to take that first step.

It's easy to romanticize success stories from the outside looking in, but every success story starts with someone who is scared and uncertain. The only difference between them and the person who let the opportunity slip away is that they took action despite their fear. They stepped out in faith, knowing they might stumble but trusting that they'd find their footing along the way.

So, what's holding you back? Is it the fear of failure? The fear of judgment? Or maybe it's the fear of the unknown? Whatever it is, remember that every opportunity you take is a chance to grow, learn, and become a better version of yourself. The path may not always be clear, but that's part of the adventure. When you step out in faith, you open yourself up to endless possibilities, and that's where the magic happens.

Opportunity is like a door. You can stand in front of it, wondering what's on the other side, worrying about whether you're ready to walk through it, or you can take a deep breath, turn the handle, and step into the unknown. Sure, there might be challenges on the other side, but there's also the chance for something amazing. You won't know until you take that first step.

Stepping out in faith doesn't mean you won't have doubts. It doesn't mean you'll have all the answers. It just means you're willing to trust the process, take the leap, and give yourself a chance to seize the opportunities that come your way. And who knows? The opportunity you take today might just lead to the breakthrough you've been waiting for.

I recall being at an international conference and minding my own business, and in my prereferral, I saw a living legend named Dennis Jackson making a B-Line Across the conference floor with two people with him. Excited and full of energy as Dennis often is, he says, "Troy, you need to go to England."

In my six seconds of silence, I had a whole conversation in my head. I think he knows exactly what I do and who I am. I am a black man who is all about equipping the church to do urban ministry. I'm thinking about where I should go and who I should go to in England. As I snapped out of the internal dialog, Dennis started to describe a Caribbean denomination that could use some encouragement and possibly some consultation on what it looks like to create a disciple-making movement.

Within a year, my wife and I were on a plane to England to watch, learn, and encourage the people here. After 48 hrs in the country, it was very clear why he wanted Me to go. These were my people! Loving and leading with hospitality as a primary value. After taking two weeks, we made our way across the country, listening, praying, and casting a vision. It was clear what I was there for.

This denomination had not planted any churches in over 50 years and was not seeing youth come to their churches and stay. This is the makeup of The Walking Dead. This means that the church's primary and most fruitful vehicle for disciple-making is the local church.

And in their case, this body that should be full of life and life-giving was bleeding out. The more I met with leaders, the more I realized they were expecting me to fix this 50-year-old issue of blood. I had mixed emotions, as on one end, my wife and I both fell in love with the people.

On the other hand, I knew I was grossly underqualified to move the needle. Like Moses, I reasoned with God... I'm uneducated, I'm an ex-felon, and I don't speak or spell well. All of my insecurities of old rushed in like a flood. It came to a head one day while sitting in my living room one day, and I was physically shaking and weeping silently. I texted mentors and accountability partners, and nothing. I was in a full panic attack at this point, and my friend and brother Donnie hit me back. I told him how I was feeling.

Maybe because of my emotional state, I do not remember his words. But I remember the presence of God coming over me. Not in a superhero endowed with great power, ready to save the day type of way. But the freedom in the fact that I don't have to be the answer, the fixer, or be enough. The feeling that God was saying who Gave you your mouth, who gave you your mind? I got up, still uncertain of what and how anything would get done.

But I was able to stand on the fact that God was gonna do something, and I was going along for the ride. I spent 2 years going back and forth to England, and by God's grace, I reinitiated the spark that these amazing people once had for reaching their community. Together, we built the infrastructure for a church planting network that is in existence to date.

So, next time you find yourself standing at a crossroads with an opportunity in front of you and fear whispering in your ear, remember this: you don't have to be fearless to take the leap—you just have to be willing. Step out in faith, and you might just surprise yourself with where you land.

GOD OVER EVERYTHING

We live in a world full of uncertainties, decisions, and pressures, where we often find ourselves struggling with control—trying to steer the ship of our lives, make the right choices, and figure out our path. But there's a level of peace that comes when we step back and realize that, in life, we're not the ones truly in control. That's where the idea of "God over everything" comes in. It's not just a phrase; it's a mindset and a lifestyle that shifts how we approach every aspect of our lives.

Putting God over everything means letting go of the need to control every outcome. It's recognizing that no matter how much we plan, strategize, or worry, God's plan is greater than ours. His understanding is beyond our own, and His timing is perfect, even when it doesn't line up with what we expected. This can be tough to grasp because, as humans, we naturally want to be the ones holding the reins. But when you step back and acknowledge that God is in control, it frees you from the pressure of having to figure everything out on your own.

Life is full of unexpected challenges. We've all had moments where things didn't go the way we planned. Maybe you didn't get that job you were hoping for, or a relationship didn't work out the way you imagined. In those moments, it's easy to feel frustrated, confused, or even defeated. But when you live with the belief that God is over everything, those disappointments take on a new perspective. Instead of seeing them as setbacks, you begin to see them as redirections—the Lord guiding you toward something better, something aligned with His will.

The truth is, we can't always see the bigger picture. We're living in the moment, and our perspective is limited to what's right in front of us. But the Lord sees the whole world. He knows how every piece fits together. When you trust that God is over everything, it allows you to release the grip you have on your life and surrender to His plan. And in that surrender, you find peace, even in the challenges.

One of the most freeing aspects of putting God over everything is that it takes the burden off your shoulders. You don't have to have all the answers. You don't have to know exactly how everything will play out. It's okay to admit that you're uncertain or that you don't have it all figured out because the Lord does. When you let go and trust Him to lead, you'll find that life becomes less about controlling outcomes and more about walking in faith.

This doesn't mean life will be perfect or free from challenges. Trusting God over everything doesn't guarantee that things will always go smoothly. But it does guarantee that, no matter what you face, the Lord is with you, guiding you and working things out for your good. Even when the road is difficult, there's comfort in knowing that you're not walking it alone.

Putting God first means aligning your priorities with His. It's about recognizing that, at the end of the day, what matters most is your relationship with Him. Everything else—your career, your goals, your aspirations—should come secondary to that. It doesn't mean those things aren't important, but they shouldn't overshadow your connection with God.

When you make God the foundation of your life, everything else falls into place. It changes how you approach your decisions, your relationships, and your challenges. You begin to ask, "Is this in line with what the Lord wants for me?" instead of, "What do I want?" This shift in perspective allows you to live in alignment with His will rather than constantly chasing after your own desires.

We live in a world that glorifies success, achievement, and personal ambition. But when you place God over everything, your focus shifts from striving for the things of this world to seeking His kingdom first. Matthew 6:33 says, "Seek first the kingdom of God and His righteousness, and all these things will be added to you." When you prioritize God's will above all else, He provides for your needs in ways that you couldn't have imagined.

Putting God over everything also means trusting Him with the things that matter most to you—your family, your career, and your dreams. It's about saying, "Jesus, I trust You with this," even when you're scared or unsure of the outcome. It's about surrendering your hopes and desires to Him, knowing that He has a better plan for your life than you could ever create on your own.

This kind of trust requires faith. It requires believing that God's plan is not only good but better than anything you could come up with. And it requires patience because God's timing is not always our timing. There will be seasons of waiting, and there will be times when you feel like you're wandering in the wilderness. But even in those moments, the Lord is working behind the scenes, setting things in motion that you can't see.

It's in those moments of waiting, of uncertainty, that faith is tested. But it's also in those moments that your relationship with the Lord grows deeper. When you put God over everything, you learn to lean on Him more, to seek His guidance, and to trust that He is with you. And when you come out on the other side, you'll see how He was orchestrating everything for your good all along.

Living with a "God over everything" mindset means recognizing that you're not in control—and that's okay. It's not about passivity or giving up on your dreams; it's about trusting that God's dreams for you are even bigger. It's about walking in faith, knowing that He's guiding your steps and leading you toward something greater.

In the end, putting God over everything brings peace that nothing else can provide. It allows you to navigate life's ups and downs with a steady heart because you know who's really in charge. When you trust God over everything, you stop trying to force things to happen and instead allow His plan to unfold in your life. And in that trust, you find true freedom.

So, the next time you're faced with a decision, a challenge, or a setback, remember to take a step back and remind yourself, "God over everything." And when He's at the helm, you're exactly where you need to be.

I SUCK, GOD IS DOPE & I NEED HIM

When Moses received his call from God, he wasn't like, "Put me in the game, coach!" Actually, he was doing everything in his power to avoid it! You remember the story, right? God basically did backflips to convince the guy to go and be who he was created to be. He was called to lead the Israelites out of bondage. I feel like Dory in Finding Nemo: "This is gonna be good, I can tell." Moses was minding his business after realizing what his calling and passion were, and now, he was working his job. He was chilling, taking care of the sheep, and minding his own business. Then he saw the bush on fire, and it started talking.

We have to give Moses some props. Most of us would have bounced the moment we saw the bush burning nonstop. But he stuck around, and then God spoke. He heard God call him from the burning bush, and you can almost hear Moses saying, "Uh, you sure you got the right dude? I've got all kinds of issues." After going back and forth with Moses, God responded in a way only He can. He didn't leave Moses hanging; He sent Aaron to go with him, to be his mouthpiece and speak what God spoke to Moses.

This story is a powerful reminder of how we often feel like we need to be the most qualified person to move on to the opportunities the

Lord has put in front of us. In this fast-paced world, where academics and credentials are often king, it's easy to fall into the trap of thinking we need to have it all figured out. And while I'm all for education and digging deep—I'm an information nut, I gotta have it!—I've learned that sometimes our search for perfection and intelligence can actually hinder us from seeking God first.

Have you ever heard the term "analysis paralysis"? I know that's the old man in me coming out again. This is one of those phrases that rings true in so many situations. We get so caught up in trying to figure everything out and weighing the options, which pushes us to overanalyze every little detail that we end up getting nothing done. Then, we become so consumed by our own abilities that we hesitate to move when God is clearly giving us a word to make a move. God is saying to us, like He said to Moses, "I am with you! I've got your back!"

The good news is this: God knows we fall short; He knows that He's dope and only requires that we seek Him like we are desperate for Him. Despite popular motivational opinion, you will never be good enough because God set the deck! He sent His best, the only one who is good enough—His Son, the King of Kings, Lord of Lords, the one and only Jesus Christ of Nazareth! Is that hitting you like it's hitting me? For those of us who often feel like we don't have it all together, this is good news! God will kick open doors of opportunity so we can explore our calling, our occupation, and our passions.

So, what does this look like in your life? Maybe you feel called to serve at your local church or get more involved in your community. Maybe you want to accept the call to outreach or youth ministry. The truth is, there are a lot of opportunities out there if we trust in His leading, do our part, and step through the doors when they are presented to us.

I can relate to Moses in so many ways. My speech is horrible, I'm administratively bad, I'm unorganized, and I want to handle bullies with great force. I can honestly say that I've always felt underqualified for every position I've applied for. I walk into spaces with a small set of skills, but I often feel like I'm drowning. And you know what? It's all good! I have learned to trust that God will go before me. All He requires is that I show up with a mindset that says, "I know what I know, I'm aware of what I don't know... and most importantly, I know who I know!" If you're dreaming of being an artist or a musician, don't let fear hold you back from God-given opportunities! Work at a music store, dive into the local art scene, volunteer at music events, or join an internship that will get you closer to your goal, your calling, and your passion.

A GOOD FIGHT? COUNT ME IN!!!

I grew up with the philosophy, "If you see a good fight worth fighting, don't sit there. Get up and do something!" Meaning if some type of injustice is keeping you up at night or you can't stop talking about it… Talk less, roll your sleeves up, and dive in headfirst! Just don't put people under the sand…

Leading up to the 2024 elections, it's a chaotic mess! I've not seen more confusion from all sides of the room in my 50+ years on this earth. To hear the confusion in young people is the most disturbing element of this discouraging. Where they don't feel like they can vote without being ostracized one way or another, but people who are supposed to be loving adults in the room are so preoccupied with their political red and blue gods that they can't see that they are tearing away at our youth and young adults one dumb comment at a time. Leaving them to see a good fight that people have died to protect and just throw their hands up.

To my people with less grey hair than me, I want to give you the freedom to Forget what these weird people are saying and doing. We need your life in the fight!!!! We need all voices and all perspectives so that we can find a greater balance than the ball of yarn those of us who have come before you have created. What happens in Washington affects us all in some way. I get it; it's so complex and full of lies and deception that we really don't know how policies and people will truly affect us until they are elected and policies are in play. With all the red tape, there is only one thing you can do. Vote your convictions and keep it moving. Maybe the greater opportunity is to get involved at the local level. Attend city council meetings, reach out to your mayor's office, or connect with your local police department. Ask them how you can serve your community better.

I'll never forget the moment I was invited to join an anti-gang task force. I thought I was once on the other side of the law, and here I was, given an opportunity to use my negative experiences to do good and help prevent others from going down that same road. At the same time, seeing police reform as they start to better understand their involvement in the community is crucial. It was a chance to be a voice for change to show how we could approach things from a place of prevention, intervention, and enforcement.

With all my issues, that wasn't the only civil opportunity that came my way. I also had the chance to serve on the advisory board for the chief of police, focusing on diversifying law enforcement in our communities. We know that sometimes, urban communities feel over-policed and misunderstood. So, we worked hard to recruit individuals from those communities who could bridge the gap. It felt surreal to step into a role where I could be part of the solution, especially given my complicated history with law enforcement.

It's really easy to think, "Oh, I can't make a difference," especially when you have a past like mine. But in real talk, God will always have the last say. He turned my life around and opened opportunities I never thought could be possible. All I had to do was trust Him and believe that He was ultimately in charge, not me.

So the next time you find yourself at the door of opportunity feeling unqualified or unsure, remember that God doesn't call the equipped; He equips the called. I promise... That's my last and final old-man quote. All I'm trying to say is... Step out in faith, embrace the opportunities before you, and watch how He uses you to have an impact in your community and beyond! You never know how stepping through that door might change not only your life but the lives of those around you. It did with Moses...

Exodus 4:10-17, "But Moses said to the Lord, "Pardon your servant, Lord. I have never been eloquent, neither in the past nor since you have spoken to your servant. I am slow of speech and tongue."

The Lord said to him, "Who gave human beings their mouths? Who makes them deaf or mute? Who gives them sight or makes them blind? Is it not I, the Lord? Now go; I will help you speak and will teach you what to say."

But Moses said, "Pardon your servant, Lord. Please send someone else."

Then the Lord's anger burned against Moses and he said, "What about your brother, Aaron the Levite? I know he can speak well. He is already on his way to meet you, and he will be glad to see you. You shall speak to him and put words in his mouth; I will help both of you speak and will teach you what to do. He will speak to the people for you, and it will be as if he were your mouth and as if you were God to him."

Life Application: God will provide the necessary opportunities for us to fulfill our purpose, but we must be the ones looking for them. This will require stepping out of our comfort zones, taking risks, or even relocating to a new spot. By keeping our eyes fixed on God, we can be confident that He will guide us to the right places and people to accomplish His will for our lives.

REFLECTION QUESTIONS

- When have you witnessed God opening unexpected doors or presenting you with opportunities that stretched your faith? How did you respond, and what did you learn in the process?

- What are some of the fears, doubts, or insecurities that have held you back from stepping out and seizing the opportunities God has placed before you? How can you overcome those obstacles?

- Who are the people in your life that have encouraged you to take bold steps of faith, even when the path ahead was uncertain? How can you cultivate more of those types of relationships?

- In what areas of your life do you feel God may be calling you to step out in faith and try something new? What specific opportunities do you sense He is placing before you?

- How can you develop a posture of openness and expectancy, actively looking for the doors God is opening rather than passively waiting for them to appear? What habits or practices can you implement to stay attuned to His leading?

GUIDE TO IDENTIFYING AND ACTING ON OPPORTUNITIES

1. Before you can identify opportunities, take stock of where you are right now.

2. What are your strengths, weaknesses, experiences, and interests?

3. Create a personal SWOT analysis (Strengths, Weaknesses, Opportunities, Threats) in your community.

4. Set aside a specific time each day to pray about your future. Ask God to help you see the opportunities He is placing in front of you.

5. Keep a prayer journal to document your thoughts and feelings during this time of seeking.

6. Approach a local church in your community and tithe 10% of the time that you have. Given to your job (4 hours per week)

7. Make a habit of reading local news, following community boards, and joining social media groups focused on your interests.

8. Set a reminder to check in with yourself weekly about your current opportunities. What have you noticed? What seems to resonate with you?

9. Reflect on past opportunities you've pursued. What did you learn from the experiences, even if they didn't turn out as you planned?

10. Write down a list of your fears regarding failure. Then, next to each fear, write down a positive outcome that could arise from stepping forward despite that fear.

11. Choose one opportunity you want to pursue and outline the steps needed to take action. Break it down into manageable tasks with deadlines.

12. Hold yourself accountable by sharing your goals with a trusted friend or mentor who can encourage you along the way.

Conclusion

As we reach the end of our journey through the COPO framework, I hope you've gotten a deeper understanding of the unique purpose God has for your life, from taking a deep dive into your calling to aligning your occupation and passions and seeking opportunities to flush them out. This process was designed to help you uncover the path He has laid out before you.

Throughout these pages, we've wrestled with tough questions and confronted the often uncomfortable realities of our lives. But the dope part of it all is that we did this work together. So, as we reflect on all that we've discovered through the COPO framework, let's take a moment to recap the key nugget we've taken away from this:

CALLING: Embrace Your Divine Purpose

At the top of the COPO is the idea of calling that God has placed in each of us with his unique purpose to fulfill. Throughout the Scriptures, we see example after example of regular people being called to do the impossible through God. From Moses to Esther, David to the Apostle Paul, the common thread is a willingness to surrender their lives to him at all costs.

As we've explored our own callings, we've had to come face-to-face with our insecurities, our shortcomings, and the areas where we feel most unqualified. But the Lord reminds us that He is not looking for greatness. He is looking for hearts that are fully surrendered to Him. When we humbly acknowledge our need for His strength and guidance, that's when He shows up And does his thing. So, I encourage you to embrace your calling with all you got!

Occupation: Find joy in the work that you do

We've taken a look at what occupation looks like in real-time. In a world that often prioritizes passion and finding the "perfect" job, it can be easy to feel dissatisfied or even unappreciative of the jobs, businesses, and mi1wnistries we have now.

However, the Scriptures see this differently. From the jump, God has ordained work as a means of glorifying Him and serving other people.

The key is recognizing that our occupations are not meant to define our identities or our ultimate purpose. Rather, they are tools that can be used to support the unique calling God has placed on our lives. Whether you're a CEO, a stay-at-home parent, or a factory worker, your work can be an act of worship when it is done with an attitude of service and a desire to honor the Lord.

Passion: Surrendering Your Desires to God

God-given desires that push us into action are passions. These are powerful forces that can either propel us forward in pursuit of our callings or lead us astray if left unchecked. Throughout the Scriptures, we see countless examples of individuals whose passions were both a blessing and a curse. Moses was driven by a "righteous" anger at the injustice he witnessed, which ultimately led him to kill an Egyptian.

The key is learning to surrender our passions to the Lord, allowing Him to refine and redirect them for His purposes. When we do this, we unlock the door to a life of greater impact and fulfillment. Our hurts become the fuel that drives us to make a difference.

I'm NOT saying that the road to finding, accepting, and acting on our passion is easy. Surrendering our passions can be extremely uncomfortable the whole way through. It requires us to let go of our own agendas and trust that God's plan is better. When we align our passions with God's purpose, we discover a joy and a sense of purpose that makes zero sense to most.

Opportunity: Stepping Out in Faith

The Scriptures outline several instances where the Lord opens doors and presents us with opportunities to step out in faith and fulfill our callings, seek work, and follow our passion. Moses, for example, was working tending sheep in the wilderness when God appeared to him in the burning bush and called him to lead the Israelites out of Egypt.

Moses was faced with a choice. He could shrink back in fear and doubt, or would he step out in faith and trust that God would equip him for the task at hand? Thankfully, Moses saw a fight, stepped up, and Jumped in!! The same is true for us today. God is constantly presenting us with opportunities to make an impact in the world around us. But all too often, we allow our insecurities, our fears, and our own limited perspectives to hold us back.

I want to encourage you to keep your eyes open for the doors God is opening in your life. Trust that the same God who called you and equipped you will also provide for you and guide you every step of the way.

FREE RESOURCE TO START REIMAGINING YOUR PURPOSE